DK EYEWITNESS

TOP **10**
ICELAND

Top 10 Iceland Highlights

The Top 10 of Everything

CONTENTS

Iceland Area by Area

Streetsmart

Within each Top 10 list in this book, no hierarchy of quality or popularity is implied. All 10 are, in the editor's opinion, of roughly equal merit.

Title page, front cover and spine Behind the picturesque Seljalandsfoss waterfall *Back cover, clockwise from top left* Sunset at Reykjavik harbour; snowboarding in Bláfjöll; aurora borealis at Kirkjufell; Seljalandsfoss waterfall; Reykjavik cityscape

Welcome to
Iceland

The land of the Vikings and their sagas, this small country never fails to enchant visitors with its mix of lunar deserts, thundering waterfalls, erupting volcanoes and majestic fjords. All this only begins to describe Iceland... so who could deny it's Europe's wildest, most rugged destination? With Eyewitness Top 10 Iceland, it's yours to explore.

Here you can spend never-ending summer days strolling **Reykjavík**'s historic centre, taking an outdoor thermal soak in the surreal waters of the **Blue Lagoon**, enjoying fresh-caught salmon or lobster in a seafront restaurant, tackling the **Laugavegur** trail between **Landmannalaugar**'s hot springs and the beautiful highland wilderness at Þórsmörk, or gazing at powder-blue icebergs drifting lazily around at **Jökulsárlón**. It's all here on this island nation, floating just below the Arctic Circle.

It is not just the country's landscape that draws visitors here. Small but sophisticated Reykjavík offers a melange of cafés, bars and museums. Whilst history and the elements are visibly entangled at sites such as **Þingvellir**, the rift-valley location of Iceland's original Viking parliament, or **Laxárdalur**, the setting for the tragic *Laxdæla Saga*. But in the end, it's Iceland's raw beauty that really captures the imagination: the smouldering lava fields, huge volcanic craters, bubbling mud pools and seething geysers.

Whether you're visiting for a weekend or a week, our Top 10 guide brings together the best of everything that Iceland has to offer, from four-wheel-drive expeditions across the Interior to gentle walks around Reykjavík's city parks. The guide has useful tips throughout, from seeking out what's free to avoiding the crowds, plus nine easy-to-follow itineraries, designed to tie together a clutch of sights in a short space of time. Add inspiring photography and detailed maps, and you've got the essential pocket-sized travel companion. **Enjoy the book, and enjoy Iceland**.

Clockwise from top: Jökulsárlón icebergs, the Blue Lagoon, Hallgrímskirkja in Reykjavík, Eyjafjallajökull volcano erupting, Vík church, a puffin, turf houses in Djúpivogur

Exploring Iceland

Iceland's attractions are split between its unique island culture and its often explosive scenery – and with many landscapes closely tied to famous historic events, you'll often find both together. Here are some ideas for making the most of your stay, whether you are here on a weekend break in Reykjavík, or have time to circuit the country.

Reykjavík's old house are weatherproofed in brightly coloured corrugated iron.

Strokkur geyser erupts every few minutes.

Þingvellir Geysir Gullfoss

Reykjavík

Kerið

Blue Selfoss
Lagoon

Hvolsvöllur Eyjafjalla
Saga Centre

Seljalandsfoss

Skógafoss

Key
— Two-day itinerary
— Seven-day itinerary

Two Days in Iceland

Day ❶
Stroll around **Reykjavík**'s midtown and harbour (see p75), taking in the **Harpa** theatre (see p76) and cultural exhibitions at **Landnámssýningin**, **Safnahúsið** and **Listasafn Íslands** (see p75). In the afternoon, survey the city from atop **Hallgrímskirkja** (see p76) or **Perlan** (see p77) before admiring Modernist canvases at **Kjarvalsstaðir** (see p76). Finish with the zoo and botanic gardens at **Laugardalur** (see p77).

Day ❷
Take a Golden Circle tour (or drive) around the ancient parliament site at Þingvellir (see pp12–13), **Geysir**'s hot pools and waterspouts (see pp16–17)

and the thundering falls of **Gullfoss** (see pp18–19). Enjoy an evening soak at the **Blue Lagoon** (see pp14–15).

Seven Days in Iceland

Day ❶
Explore **Reykjavík**'s historic midtown and harbour (see p75), taking in the excellent, subterranean **Landnámssýningin** exhibition (see p75). Drive around the iconic landscapes at Þingvellir (see pp12–13), **Geysir** (see pp16–17) and **Gullfoss** (see pp18–19), before heading past **Kerið** crater (see p112) to spend the night in the town of Selfoss.

Day ❷
Travel the southwest coast, via the **Hvolsvöllur Saga Centre** (see p112),

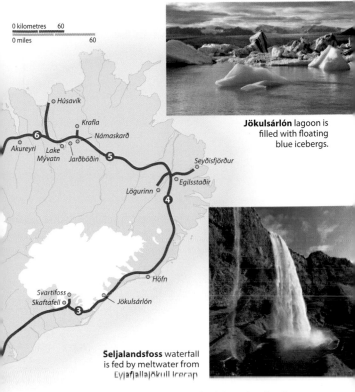

0 kilometres   60

0 miles   60

Jökulsárlón lagoon is filled with floating blue icebergs.

Seljalandsfoss waterfall is fed by meltwater from Eyjafjallajökull icecap.

the waterfall at **Seljalandsfoss** (see p44), the striking **Eyjafjallajökull** icecap (see p46) – site of the 2010 eruption – and **Skógafoss** (see p45). Stay overnight at **Vík** (see p110), with its teeming seabird colonies.

Day ❸

Cross the gravel desert that lies east of Vík to **Skaftafell** (see p25), where you can see glacier tongues and the **Svartifoss** waterfall (see p54). Continue to the icebergs at **Jökulsárlón** (see pp32–3) and lobster restaurants at **Höfn** (see p103), with views of the **Vatnajökull** icecap (see p24) along the way.

Day ❹

Travel up the east coast and then inland to **Egilsstaðir** (see p101), where you could either circuit

Lögurinn lake or head to the picturesque East Fjords port of **Seyðisfjörður** (see p102).

Day ❺

Drive towards **Lake Mývatn** (see pp20–21), detouring to explore the Krafla eruption site and Námaskarð's mud pools. Circuit Lake Mývatn before unwinding at Jarðböðin Nature Baths.

Day ❻

Head to the north coast for a whale-watching trip out of **Húsavík** (book in advance; see p96), before driving to pleasant **Akureyri** (see p96).

Day ❼

Return to Reykjavík and spend a couple of hours at the **Blue Lagoon** (see pp14–15) en route to the airport.

Top 10 Iceland Highlights

Jökulsárlón lagoon at sunset

🔟 Iceland Highlights

Iceland sits on an active volcanic ridge at the edge of the Arctic Circle. Only birds and foxes inhabited the land when Vikings arrived in the 8th century to found the commonwealth of the Saga Age. Towns were not established until the 18th century. Today, it has a hi-tech infrastructure and most of its 320,000 population lives around Reykjavík.

Þingvellir National Park ①

This broad rift valley, where the tectonic plates are visibly tearing apart in a riot of geology, was the site of Iceland's Viking parliament (see pp12–13).

② The Blue Lagoon

Take a sauna or soak in the pale blue waters of Iceland's most sublime outdoor spa set among black lava boulders (see pp14–15).

③ Geysir Hot Springs Area

Just an hour from Reykjavík, this hillside of bubbling pools and erupting waterspouts has given its name to similar formations around the world (see pp16–17).

Gullfoss ④

This powerful water-fall has been a national symbol since it was saved from oblivion during the 1920s (see pp18–19).

• Ísafjörður   • Gjögur
Þingeyri
Bíldudalur
                 Hólmavík
Látrabjarg ⑧   • Brjánslækur
Bird Cliffs   Laugar
        Breiðafjörður
Ólafsvík   • Stykkishólmur   • Brú
        ⑦ • Vegamót
Snæfellsjökull   • Bifröst
National Park
        Borgarnes   Lang
  Faxaflói   Þingvellir   Gullfoss
              National Park ①   ③
        Reykjavík •   Geysir H
The Blue   Springs A
Lagoon ②   • Selfoss
              Hvolsvöllur

⑤ Lake Mývatn Area

Lake Mývatn is home to the best of Iceland in one place: wildfowl, volcano cones, mud pits, steaming lava flows and thermal pools (see pp20–21).

Vatnajökull National Park

This reserve protects not only the Vatnajökull icecap and its out-running glaciers, but also beautiful rivers, gorges and mountain formations (see pp24–5).

Snæfellsjökull National Park

Western Iceland's peninsula peaks with the snowy cone of Snæfellsjökull, a slumbering volcano crossed by hiking trails. It is tall enough to be visible from Reykjavík (see pp26–7).

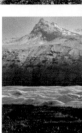

Látrabjarg Bird Cliffs

Fantastically remote even by Icelandic standards, north-westerly Látrabjarg supports one of the largest seabird colonies in Europe, and is home to millions of gulls, guillemots and puffins (see pp28–9).

Kópasker
Þórshöfn
Siglufjörður
Bakkafjörður
Dalvík
Vopnafjörður
Bárkrókur
Reykjahlíð
Grímsstaðir
Akureyri
Lake Mývatn Area
Borgarfjörður Eystri
Egilsstaðir
Hofsjökull
Eskifjörður
Djúpivogur
Vatnajökull
Vatnajökull National Park
Höfn
Landmannalaugar Area
Skaftafell
Jökulsárlón
Fagurhólsmýri
gar
Vík

0 km 60
0 miles 60

Jökulsárlón

Travel along the Ringroad to this lagoon between the Breiðamerkurjökull glacier and the Atlantic Ocean, which is full of seals and icebergs (see pp32–3).

Landmannalaugar Area

Its bridgeless rivers, shattered grey mountains and hot springs make you feel like an explorer in the wild, but summer buses make this area easily accessible for visitors (see pp30–31).

TOP 10 ⭐ Þingvellir National Park

Iceland's location on the mid-Atlantic ridge is obvious at Þingvellir (Assembly Plains), where the land has crashed in a deep scar stretching north from Lake Þingvallavatn. In AD 930, this dramatic setting was chosen by the island's 36 chieftains as the site of their annual Alþing (General Assembly). Almost 4,000 of the country's 60,000 inhabitants gathered here to hear laws and to settle disputes, occasionally by combat. The Alþing's power declined after Iceland accepted Norwegian sovereignty in 1262, but the assembly continued to be held here until 1798.

① Lögberg

A prominent outcrop below Almannagjá's cliffs marks the site where the Alþing's Lawspeaker stood and recited the country's laws to the masses below. Look nearby for faint outlines of *buðir*, the tented camps used during Viking times.

② Þingvellir Church

This surprisingly low-key wooden building with a black roof **(below)** is a reminder of the Alþing of AD 1000, when, despite strong opposition from pagan priests, the Icelandic nation adopted Christianity as its sole religion under threat of Norwegian invasion *(see p36)*. The church was built in 1859 but it has a pulpit that dates back to 1683.

③ Volcanic Features

The broad, flattened dome of northerly Skjaldbreiður – an ancient shield volcano – was the source of the lava flow now covering Þingvellir's valley. Cut by deep fissures, the lava cooled into rough *a'a* outcrops and pavements of smoother *pahoehoe* (both of which are types of lava).

④ Almannagjá

A walk through Almannagjá's deep, cliff-lined gully **(above)** is a good way to appreciate Þingvellir's geology. Here, as the North American and European continental plates drift apart at a rate of 2.5 cm (1 inch) a year, Iceland is literally ripping in half.

⑤ Þingvallavatn

At 84 sq km (33 sq miles), Þingvallavatn **(below)** is the largest natural lake in Iceland. Its clear waters are famous for char and trout fishing, as well as scuba diving.

⑨ Flora
Þingvellir valley's floor is covered in a thick carpet of moss, lichen, orchids, dwarf willow and birch. Visit in autumn for exceptional colours and join the locals in picking crowberries (left), which are used to make jam.

⑥ Drekkingarhylur
Legend has it that the Öxaráfoss falls were created when the river was diverted in around AD 930 to provide drinking water during the assemblies. In medieval times, executions were carried out here.

⑦ Wildlife
The area just to the north of Þingvallavatn's lakeshore abounds in interesting wildlife. Keep an eye out for swans, mergansers (right) and northern divers on the water, as well as snipes, ptarmigans, minks and Arctic foxes on land.

⑧ Visitor Centre
Perched atop the western side of the rift, on Route 36, the Visitor Centre offers superb views of Þingvellir. It also shows multilingual films and has a range of DVDs on the region's geology and history.

⑩ Peningagjá
Peningagjá is an extraordinary sight: a narrow but deep lava fissure flooded with clear, peacock-blue water. At the bottom of this well you can see the glinting coins left by hopeful visitors.

PAYING THE PENALTY

Law courts at the Alþing strangely had no power to enforce their judgments. Litigants accepted the verdicts because they reflected public opinion, but in theory – and sometimes in practice – powerful men could ignore the sentences against them. The courts tried to resolve serious disputes through mediation, but some were sentenced to the highest Viking penalty, which was to be outlawed (banished from Iceland) for 20 years and then killed.

NEED TO KNOW

MAP C5 ▪ From Reykjavík, Golden Circle tour buses visit Þingvellir daily year-round; some 6 and 6a buses and summer services using the Kjölur route also stop here; if driving, allow 60–90 minutes via Route 36 ▪ Bus schedule: www.bsi.is ▪ www.thingvellir.is/english

▪ From the Visitor Centre, through Almannagjá, descend to the Law Rock. Take a detour to see Peningagjá and the church, then walk up to Drekkingarhylur. In good weather, follow hiking tracks up the rift to some abandoned farms, but take care as the dense undergrowth hides deep fissures.

▪ The Visitor Centre at Hakið sells sandwiches, whilst the service centre sells soups and pizza.

🔟 ⭐ The Blue Lagoon and Around

The Blue Lagoon (*Bláa Lónið*) is Iceland's premier geothermal spa and one of the country's most beautiful. Set in a desolate lava wilderness, the lagoon's bright blue waters add a surreal splash of colour. You can laze in the steaming waters, have a beauty treatment, enjoy an excellent meal or stay nearby and catch the seasonal display of the aurora borealis. If you have your own transport, consider taking a detour to see some unusual sights, including Grindavík's Saltfish Museum, the Seltún Hot Springs and Selatangar's abandoned fishing camp.

1 Background and Origin
The Blue Lagoon was created when superheated seawater flowing out of the Svartsengi Geothermal Power Station collected in the surrounding lava **(above)**. Locals discovered that a warm dip cured skin ailments and public facilities opened here during the 1980s.

2 Unique Lava Setting
The lagoon is bordered by rough masses of black lava boulders, which lie piled high around the perimeter, hemming in the powder-blue waters.

3 Geothermal Spa
The water, at a temperature of 37°C (99°F), is comfortable and the huge pool **(below)** is an amazing place to unwind, with an adjacent sauna.

4 Spa Services
Enjoy a relaxing massage in a private area of the lagoon itself **(above)**, or opt for a cleansing rub-down using the naturally processed fine silica, minerals, algae and salt distilled from the Blue Lagoon's waters. Beauty treatments are also available. It is a good idea to book any spa treatments in advance.

5 Dermatology and Health Clinics
The Blue Lagoon's mineral salts and silica have long enjoyed a reputation for quickly curing eczema, psoriasis and other skin problems. You can seek specialized treatment while staying at the clinic near the lagoon or simply buy products that you can use at home.

6 LAVA Restaurant

Enjoy Icelandic dishes, such as grilled lobster with garlic butter or fillet of lamb, with a view of the lagoon from your table. There's also an excellent bar accessible from the water and a café selling snacks.

7 Icelandic Saltfish Museum

At Grindavík, a short drive south, is this eccentric museum (left) that traces the fishing heritage of Iceland through dioramas and photographs.

GEOTHERMAL POWER

Svartsengi Geothermal Power Station takes advantage of its location over a fault line to provide cheap, green power and hot water for the Reykjanes Peninsula. Seawater is pumped over 1 km (0.6 miles) underground, turns to steam and is used to drive the turbines that help produce 76 MW of electricity. The steam is then cooled and released into the Blue Lagoon. Five geothermal plants produce a quarter of the nation's electricity.

10 Overnight Stay

Accommodation options for overnight stay include the Blue Lagoon Retreat (see p129) and the Northern Lights Inn. The latter is a particularly fantastic spot during the winter, when the colourful aurora borealis can at times be seen playing across the night sky.

8 Seltún Hot Springs

About 22 km (13 miles) east of the lagoon are the Seltún Hot Springs (below). One of the geysers exploded in 1999. Walk the boardwalk to explore the steaming vents.

9 Selatangar

This village 15 km (9 miles) from the lagoon was abandoned in the 1850s. Ruins are visible through black sand dunes and lava outcrops.

NEED TO KNOW

MAP B5 ■ The Blue Lagoon, 240 Grindavík ■ Several tour buses daily from Reykjavík's BSÍ station; bus information: www.re.is ■ 420 8800 ■ www.bluelagoon.com

Open Jan–May: 8am–10pm daily; Jun: 7am 11pm daily; Jul–Aug: 7am–midnight daily; Sep: 8am–10pm daily; Oct–Dec: 8am–8pm daily

Adm: ISK6,100–26,500 (pre-booking essential)

Icelandic Saltfish Museum: www.grindavik.is
Seltún Hot Springs: www.visitreykjanes.is
Selatangar: www.visitreykjanes.is

■ The Blue Lagoon's high mineral content can damage your hair – condition before a swim and shampoo thoroughly afterwards.

■ Apart from the main restaurant, there is a basic café at the Blue Lagoon's entrance where you can buy coffee, cold drinks and snacks.

🔟 ⭐ Geysir Hot Springs Area

The Geysir Hot Springs area lies on the lower slopes of Bjarnarfell, 90 minutes northeast of Reykjavík, and comprises a dozen or more hot water blowholes, including Geysir, the spout that gave its name to other geysers worldwide. The area became active about 1,000 years ago and today the most impressive spout is Strokkur, which you will definitely see in action. Geysir's pool is far larger but count yourself lucky if you see more than bubbles. Visit Haukadalur for an interesting old church and some undemanding hiking.

① Geysir Hot Spring
Geysir, "the Gusher" **(above)**, has not erupted to its full 70-m (230-ft) height since the mid-20th century, though until it was banned in the 1980s, dumping soap powder into the pool used to trigger a hiccup or two.

② Blesi
Up the slope behind the Geysir area, Blesi, "the Blazer" **(below)**, is a set of twin pools, one clear and scalding; the other cooler, opaque and powder blue with dissolved minerals.

④ Strokkur
Strokkur, "the Churn" **(above)**, reliably erupts ten times per hour, its clear blue pool exploding in a 15 to 30 m- (50 to 100 ft-) high spout with little noise. In between eruptions, watch the water sighing and sinking as the pressure builds.

⑤ Litli Geysir
Often overlooked on the way to Strokkur, Litli Geysir **(below)** is off the path to the left. It was likely once a waterspout that blew itself apart, and is now a violently slushing muddy pool, belching steam and bubbles.

③ Konungshver
Catch the "King's Spring" on a sunny day and the colours are stunning. The clear, vivid blue water sits in a depression of orange-red rock. Get views from here of the rest of the Geysir area.

⑥ Hótel Geysir

Located across the road from the Geysir hot spring, this hotel **(above)** houses an indoor spa which will reopen in 2020 after renovation. The restaurant *(see p113)* offers buffet lunch and an evening menu.

⑦ Haukadalur Church

This charming red-roofed church lies in a woodland about 2 km (1 mile) behind Geysir. It was built in the 1840s and expanded in the 1930s. The ring on the door is believed to have been given to a local farmer by a giant, Bergþór, whose burial mound lies nearby.

THERE SHE BLOWS!

Geysers are formed in deep, vertical, flooded vents known as pipes. The water at the bottom of the pipe comes into contact with hot rock and boils, expanding upwards, while the cooler water at the surface of the geyser forms a kind of lid, trapping the rising water, until so much pressure builds up that the geyser explodes skywards. Watch Strokkur and you can clearly see this lid of cooler water bulging upwards just before each eruption.

⑧ Haukadalur Forest

Since the 1940s, Iceland's forestry service has planted millions of larches, pine and rowan trees in the Haukadalur valley. An easy walking trail through the area passes through a gully full of waterfalls.

NEED TO KNOW

MAP C5 ■ The Geysir area is right by the roadside on Route 35, about 90 min from Reykjavík ■ Tour buses are available from Reykjavík's BSÍ station. Bus schedule: www.bsi.is

Hótel Geysir: www.geysircenter.com

■ Stay on boardwalks or marked trails and do not step into pools or their outflows, as the water is boiling hot. Falling spray from Strokkur is cool, but you will need a raincoat if you are standing downwind.

■ The Geysir Centre has a café that serves coffee, hot dogs, drinks and sandwiches, but the hotel restaurant, although pricier, actually offers better value for money.

⑨ Geysir Centre

Directly across the road from the hot springs, the Geysir Centre has a souvenir shop **(right)** selling postcards, clothing made from Icelandic wool and unique jewellery, as well as an excellent *supa* (soup restaurant).

⑩ Bjarnarfell

It takes a steep hike to reach the 727 m (2,385 ft) summit of Bjarnarfell, the hill overlooking Geysir, but the rewards on a good day are spectacular views of the red-brown rock and green fields surrounding the springs.

🔟⭐ Gullfoss

The powerful two-tier waterfalls at Gullfoss on the Hvítá river present a stunning sight, whether part-frozen in winter, in full flood during the spring melt, or roaring away during the long summer twilight. Their setting in a deep canyon adds to the spectacle, as does the landscape of icy peaks and gravel desert immediately north – quite a contrast to the green, spray-fed vegetation closer to the river. Take care at Gullfoss and always supervise children, as paths are slippery and there are no safety railings or warning signs.

1 Origin of Names
The clouds of rainbow-tinged spray hanging over it gave Gullfoss its name – the Golden Falls. Hvítá (White River) is named after the light-coloured glacial sediment it carries.

2 Geology
The area's volcanic history can be seen on the cliffs opposite the viewing platform, with their distinct banded ash layers from separate volcanic eruptions, over-laid with basalt **(above)**.

3 The Canyon
The canyon continues downstream from Gullfoss for 2 km (1 mile), through basalt columns. You can follow the track along the top or take a white-water rafting trip.

5 View from the Top
The main viewing area, and the safest, is the platform on the top of the canyon **(above)**. Orient yourself and take in the dramatic setting.

View from Below 4
Soaked by the spray, you can really appre-ciate the sheer scale of the waterfalls **(right)** from this vantage point: the river drops 10 m (33 ft), turns a right angle and then drops again.

7 Plaque for Sigríður Tómasdóttir

A commemorative plaque to Sigríður Tómasdóttir **(left)** recalls her successful campaign to save these waterfalls from being drowned by a dam project.

6 Sigríðarstofa

The local exhibition centre, Sigríðarstofa, showcases the hardships of traditional life in the area, which is caught between relatively fertile plains to the west and the sterile wilderness of Iceland's frozen Interior directly north.

SAVING GULLFOSS

In 1907, landowner Einar Benediktsson signed away Gullfoss to be submerged by the construction of a hydro-electric dam across the Hvítá river. Sigríður Tómasdóttir, whose father was involved in the deal, was so incensed that she took legal action against the developers. Although she lost the case, public opinion ran so high in her favour that construction never began and Gullfoss was later donated to the nation of Iceland as a special reserve.

8 Visitor Centre

The roomy cafeteria at the Gullfoss Visitor Centre serves delicious, hearty food. The falls are invisible from here but the views show mountains and glaciers.

9 Souvenir Shop

The gift shop at the Visitor Centre sells nothing specific to Gullfoss apart from postcards, but it is still a good place to find T-shirts, designer outdoor gear, books on Iceland and lava jewellery.

NEED TO KNOW

MAP D4 ■ Daily tour buses from Reykjavík's BSÍ station. www.bsi.is

■ Visit in winter when Gullfoss is partly frozen and hidden behind spectacular ice curtains; in summer, the afternoon provides the best lighting conditions for photographs.

■ Make sure you try the traditional lamb soup at the Visitor Centre café – and the refills are free.

10 Kjölur

This 160-km- (100-mile-) long route **(above)**, runs north from here across the Interior, traversing the gravel plains between the Langjökull and Hofsjökull icecaps.

🔟 ⭐ Lake Mývatn Area

Known as Midge Lake in English, Mývatn is a peaceful spread of water east of Akureyri and home to flocks of wildfowl in summer. The surrounding landscape, however, is anything but tranquil, with Mývatn hemmed in by a spectacular mix of extinct cinder cones and twisted lava formations, hot bathing pools, boiling mud pits and screaming volcanic vents. North-shore Reykjahlíð is Mývatn's main settlement, where you can organize tours to local sights and also to the Askja caldera in the barren Interior.

1 Lake Mývatn

Spring-fed and covering 36 sq km (14 sq miles), Lake Mývatn was created during volcanic activity about 4,000 years ago. Lava formations dominate the northern and eastern sides of the lake, while the rest of the shoreline is marshy.

2 Pseudocraters

Looking like bonsai volcanoes, pseudocraters (below) were formed by steam blisters popping through hot lava as it flowed over marshland. There are plenty of pseudocraters around Mývatn but the best, covered in walking tracks, are at Skútustaðir.

3 Laxá

Laxá, or the Salmon River, drains out of Lake Mývatn and then runs to the sea near Húsavík. Walk along its banks to see harlequin ducks tumbling in the rough waters between May and July.

4 Dimmuborgir

This weird, tumbled mass of indescribably contorted lava formations makes for an eerie hour-long wander on marked paths. Make sure you visit the drained lava tube known as Kirkja ("the Church") and keep your eyes open for the rare and endangered gyrfalcons.

5 Waterfowl Crossroads

Insect larvae and algae in Mývatn's shallow waters provide abundant food for phalaropes, swans, divers, Slavonian grebes and 13 species of duck, including the rare Barrow's goldeneye (below), which breeds in the lake from May to August.

6 Jarðböðin Nature Baths

Like the Blue Lagoon *(see pp14–15)*, Jarðböðin **(above)** offers the chance to steam in the open-air, mineral-rich geothermal waters. The views here – of the lake and volcanic setting – are even better.

KRAFLA FIRES

Earthquakes between 1975 and 1984 opened up a long volcanic fissure at Leirhnjúkur, just west of Krafla volcano, an event that became known as the Krafla Fires. Lava poured out over the plain here, leaving behind a fascinating expanse of still-smoking formations that you can reach and explore on foot from Krafla. It is not an excursion for the faint-hearted, however, as the paths are rough and you need to be careful to avoid some dangerously hot spots.

10 Krafla

Located northeast of Mývatn, Krafla volcano last erupted during the 1720s, when its lava nearly consumed Reykjahlíð's church. Víti, Krafla's flooded crater, is bright blue **(left)**.

7 Hverfjall

This 400-m- (1,312-ft-) high cinder cone is made up of volcanic ash and gravel. There are fantastic views from the well-marked path around the crater's rim.

8 Askja

To the south of Mývatn is Askja *(see p47)*, an 8-km- (5-mile-) wide flooded caldera. The Víti crater nearby exploded in 1875, causing a virtual exodus of the northeast.

9 Námaskarð

Among a landscape of red clay with yellow and white streaks, Námaskarð is an area of violently bubbling, sulphurous mud pits **(below)**. Take great care as you explore.

NEED TO KNOW

MAP F2–3 ▪ There are local buses and tours from Akureyri ▪ There is also an airstrip at Reykjahlíð

▪ In summer you will need to buy face netting from local stores to protect yourself from irritating – though mostly harmless – swarms of tiny flies. They are worse on windless days.

▪ The Gamli Bærinn bistro-bar at Reykjahlíð serves good coffee and food. Other options for cafés around the lake include The Bird Museum, Café Sel and Kaffi Borgir.

Following pages Dettifoss waterfall cascading into the Jökulsárgljúfur canyon

🔟⭐ Vatnajökull National Park

Vatnajökull National Park covers around 14,140 sq km (5,460 sq miles), 14 per cent of Iceland's surface, and comprises the Vatnajökull icecap and disconnected areas around its fringes. The long canyons and enormous waterfalls at Jökulsárgljúfur, Skaftafell's high moorland and paired glaciers, Snæfell's wilderness and the remains of Lakagígar's catastrophic volcanic event can keep you occupied for days. Hiking, ice-climbing, snowmobiling and kayaking are among the activities possible within this huge park.

1 Vatnajökull
Europe's largest icecap by volume, Vatnajökull dominates the views inland from the south. A dozen or more outlet glaciers slide coastwards off its top **(below)**. Five active volcanoes smoulders away underneath.

2 Glacial Features
Glaciers are slow-moving rivers of ice advancing just a few centimetres a day (though most of Iceland's are shrinking). Extreme pressure grinds down underlying rock to leave gravel moraine ridges and squeezes out the air, giving them their blue colour.

3 Birdlife
Sandar, or beaches of black sand washed out from beneath Iceland's glaciers, provide nesting grounds for numerous birds, including the greater skua **(left)**, an aggressive brown seabird that sometimes preys on weaker birds and their young.

4 Hvannadalshnúkur
Protruding from Vatnajökull's icecap at 2,110 m (6,923 ft), this peak is Iceland's highest point. You need considerable experience to undertake the 15-hour trek to its summit.

5 Ásbyrgi
This gorge **(above)** is said to be a hoof print left by the Norse god Óðin's eight-legged horse, Sleipnir. Geologists say floods from Vatnajökull carved it.

6 Lakagígar

This 25-km (16-mile) row of craters **(below)** was created by a terrible eruption in 1783. Lava and poisonous gas wiped out farms in the Kirkjubæjarklaustur area, causing a nation-wide famine (see p116).

8 Skaftafell

Do not miss Svartifoss **(left)**, a waterfall framed by hexagonal basalt col-umns, in this national park that extends over 1,700 sq km (657 sq miles) of accessible highland plateau. Other highlights of this park include close-ups of blue gla-cier tongues streaked in gravel and super-lative hiking along marked trails.

FLASH FLOOD

Jökulhlaups (glacial flash floods) can happen when geothermal heating from volcanoes under the icecaps melts enough water to form a lake. If the lake dam gives way, the water explodes outwards with potentially devastating results. A single prehistoric *jökulhlaup* carved out the Jökulsárgljúfur canyon, while a smaller event in 1996 sent water rushing out from under the Vatnajökull icecap, sweeping away 7 km (5 miles) of the highway near Skaftafell.

9 Jökulsárgljúfur

The name of this national park means "Glacier River Canyon", a reference to the 120-m- (394-ft-) deep and 500-m- (1,640-ft-) wide slash through which flows Jökulsá, Iceland's second-longest river.

7 Fjallsárlón

Although smaller and less dramatic than Jökulsárlón, the Fjallsárlón glacier lagoon is just as photogenic, with its stunning floating icebergs.

10 Dettifoss

Said to be Europe's most powerful waterfall (see p97), Dettifoss **(below)** sits amidst a jagged grey basalt landscape, its 45-m (148-ft) drop sending clouds of spray skywards. Summer-only access is via the paved road 862 from road 1.

NEED TO KNOW

MAP F4 ■ Buses from Akureyri to Ásbyrgi and Dettifoss; from Reykjavík and Höfn to Skaftafell; from Kirkjubæjarklaustur and Höfn to Lakagígar ■ Tours to Vatnajökull by Jeep and snowmobile from Höfn ■ www.vatna jokulsthjodgardur.is

■ Hvannadalshnúkur and Lónsöræfi are accessible only to expert hikers.

■ Most sections of Vatnajökull National Park are completely inaccessible in winter, sometimes closed due to bad weather. Plan a trip between July and mid-August to visit a greater number of places.

■ There are few places to eat within the park, so make sure you stock up on refreshments from the nearest town.

TOP 10 ⭐ Snæfellsjökull National Park

Established in 2001, Snæfellsjökull National Park protects the snowy snout of the Snæfellsnes Peninsula, which juts 70 km (44 miles) into the sea from the western coast. Just two hours drive from Reykjavík with a beautiful conical volcano at its core, Snæfellsjökull is a place steeped in ancient, literary and New Age folklore, though most people who visit today are more interested in the mountain's hiking or climbing potential. Snæfellsjökull also makes a splendid backdrop for delving into the area's fishing history or for bird-watching.

1 Snæfellsjökull
Snæfellsjökull is the 1,445-m- (4,745-ft-) high icecap covering the dormant volcano, which last erupted in AD 250. The white cone of the volcano (below) is clearly visible to the north of Reykjavík on a clear day, rising up above Faxaflói Bay.

2 Coastal Boundary
The rugged coast of the Snæfellsnes Peninsula acts as a barrier between the rougher weather to the north and the generally drier, sunnier south. Strong storms with snowfall on the higher ground may occur throughout the year.

3 Djúpalónssandur
A pretty pebble beach near Dritvík (above), where four heavy stones – "Useless", "Half-Strength", "Puny" and "Full-Strength" – were once used to test the brawn of applicants for fishing boat crews.

4 Hellnar
Home town (left) of an Icelandic woman, Guðríður Þorbjarnardóttir, who travelled widely in the Middle Ages – as far as Greenland, Rome and America.

5 Dritvík
Some 24 km (15 miles) from Hellissandur, for centuries this bay harboured what was once the busiest fishing fleet in the area. It is a good place to take a break and reflect upon changing times.

6 Bird-Watching

Large white-tailed sea eagles **(above)** are occasionally seen in the vicinity of Snæfellsjökull National Park, although these rare birds mainly inhabit the Westfjords. The coastline also supports the usual seabirds and wildfowl.

9 Ascending Snæfellsjökull

Experienced hikers can spend a day climbing Snæfellsjökull and enjoy the view from the top. It is also possible to sled up and ski down the mountain. However, neither of these activities should be attempted without the assistance of a guide. Get advice from the Visitor Centre or the National Park office before starting the hike.

JOURNEY TO THE CENTRE OF THE EARTH

Snæfellsjökull sprang to fame in Jules Verne's novel *Journey to the Centre of the Earth*, in which a German professor and his nephew decode an ancient manuscript and use the instructions to descend into Snæfellsjökull's crater on a subterranean journey of exploration. Such craters were traditionally feared here as the literal entrances to hell, a belief that left many mountains unscaled till the 19th century.

10 Bárður's Statue

A terrific split stone statue of folk figure Bárður Snæfellsás stands near Arnarstapi. According to legend, Bárður was an early settler in the area and his protective spirit still lives on Snæfell and watches over the village.

7 Hiking the National Park

From Hellissandur, several circular hiking trails explore the lava fields and coastline west of Snæfellsjökull. Expect to encounter little beaches, rugged seascapes, rare plants, birdlife and seals.

8 Arnarstapi

Set at the foot of Snæfellsjökull's southeast corner, Arnarstapi **(below)** is a tiny fishing village, where a rocky arch known as Gatklettur stretches out to sea. Snowcat Tours, which organizes hiking tours, is situated closeby in Stóri Kambur.

NEED TO KNOW

MAP A4 ■ Buses from Reykjavík to Hellissandur: www.bsi.is, www.straeto.is ■ www.ust.is

Snæfellsjökull National Park's main office: Klettsbúð 7, Hellissandur; 436 6860; www.snaefellsjokull.is; check website for opening times

Visitor Centre: Malarrif; open May–Oct: 10am–5pm daily, Nov–Apr: 11am–4pm Mon–Fri

■ To climb Snæfellsjökull you need ice axes, crampons and weatherproof gear. Talk to National Park officers about your route and the weather conditions.

■ Hellissandur's Gilbakki serves a tasty fish soup.

Látrabjarg Bird Cliffs

The Látrabjarg bird cliffs are just about as remote a place as you can readily reach in Iceland. Traditionally a farming area, the region has become almost depopulated since the 1960s, leaving Látrabjarg to the millions of seabirds that return here to breed during the summer months. Most people come to the cliffs to see the abundant numbers of charismatic puffins. On the way there is also a worthwhile folk museum and an amazing beach at Breiðavík – probably the last thing you would expect to find in this part of the world.

1 Látrabjarg Cliffs

The 14-km- (9-mile-) long and 440-m- (1,444-ft-) high cliffs **(below)** form a colossal bird colony with millions of sea-birds including puffins, cormorants, kittiwakes, razorbills and guillemots, nesting here every year.

2 Geology

Iceland's western extremity is home to its oldest geological formations. Each distinct band of the layered cliffs – clearly visible despite the birdlife – records a different volcanic event of the past.

3 Bird Apartments

Species nest at different heights, forming banded apartments: puffins at the top, then razorbills, fulmars and kittiwakes **(below)**, with guillemots on the sheer cliff ledges.

4 Puffins

The most amiable residents of Látrabjarg are the puffins **(above)**. These small seabirds have orange feet and multicoloured, sail-shaped bills. They nest in grassy burrows at the top of the cliffs and often tolerate being approached, but do be cautious.

5 Eggs

Due to their habit of favouring crowded, sheer cliffs as places for nesting, guillemot eggs are conical – a shape that protects the precious cargo contained within them by causing the shells to roll in a circular movement around their tip rather than rolling over the edge.

Guano (6)

You cannot fail to notice the strong smell of guano, or dried bird droppings, in the air at Látrabjarg. The thick, spongy grass that grows at the top of the cliffs **(right)** exists thanks to centuries of fertile guano deposits. Without them, the puffins would not have anywhere to dig their nests.

THE WRECK OF THE SARGON

In 1947 a British trawler, *Dhoon*, foundered off the Látrabjarg coast in a December storm. Locals scrambled down the frozen cliffs, fired a safety line onto the vessel and winched the seamen to safety. The following year a film crew arrived to make a documentary about the event when another British vessel, *Sargon*, ran aground: the crew were again saved and the whole event was filmed for real.

Látrabjarg History (7)

The Látrabjarg cliffs were, until 1926, a favourite summer haunt for local farmers, who would scale the cliffs to collect bird eggs. Puffins were once caught and eaten in large numbers, a practice that continues to this day in the southern islands of Vestmannaeyjar *(see p110)*.

Bjargtangar (8)

This westernmost point of Europe is marked by the lonely beacon of the Bjargtangar lighthouse **(right)**, a small, whitewashed and distinctly weather-beaten building perched high up on the grassy clifftop. The light-house, which was built in 1948, marks the beginning of the Látrabjarg cliffs. The tower is not open to the public, but the views from the site are stunning.

NEED TO KNOW

MAP A2 ■ Summer-only buses run three days a week from Patreksfjörður (see website for details) ■ Book in advance: 456 5006; www.wa.is

Visitor Centre: Egils Ólafsson Folk Museum; 456 1511; open Jun–Sep: 10am–6pm daily

Hnjótur Museum: 456 1569; open end-May–mid-Sep: 10am–6pm daily, by appointment at other times; www.westfjords.is

■ The Látrabjarg road is rough gravel, open only in summer. Check your car rental policy. Unless you have experience of similar driving conditions, it is best to take the bus.

■ This area is remote. The hotel at Breiðavík is the nearest place for a meal.

Hnjótur Museum (9)

About 24 km (15 miles) from Látrabjarg, this isolated museum gives an insight into the lives of farmers. Do not miss the video of the *Sargon* shipwreck and the aircraft display.

Breiðavík (10)

Breiðavík, 15 km (9 miles) from Látrabjarg, features a long, golden beach **(below)** – a rarity here as the sand is usually volcanic black. On a sunny day you can almost imagine yourself in the Mediterranean.

𝗧𝗢𝗣 𝟭𝟬 ⭐ Landmannalaugar Area

Landmannalaugar, meaning "Countryman's Bathing Pool", is a lush hot springs area in southern Iceland, surrounded by a stark wilderness of snow-streaked mountains, ancient lava fields and flat glacial river valleys. Much of the countryside here has been shaped by Hekla, the country's second most active volcano. Excellent camping facilities make it a great spot from which to appreciate the rugged Interior. It is connected by summer-only buses from Reykjavík. You can also hike here along the exceptional Laugavegur trail.

1 Hot Springs
The hot springs emerge into a meadow from underneath a 15th-century lava flow, where they then mingle with a cooler stream. Wade or swim up this stream **(above)** until the water temperature increases, then sit down to enjoy a soak.

2 Mountains
Bláhnúkur, the main peak overlooking the springs, is 945-m-(3,100-ft-) high. There is an hour-long trail to its peak. From there you can view the medieval lava field and ever-changing colours of the grey, pink and orange rhyolite hills **(right)**.

3 Ófærufoss
A beautiful, two-stage water-fall **(left)** bridged by lava flowing through what looks like a small volcanic crater *(see p45)*. Do not get too close to the rim as the soil is soft.

5 Laugavegur
This long and rewarding trail from Landmannalaugar to Þórsmörk spans a distance of 60 km (37 miles), features volcanic plains, green hills, snowbound plateaus and freezing rivers. You can camp or use bunkhouses for shelter along the way.

4 Campsite
The campsite, with grassy spots by the stream and pitches on soft gravel, has showers, toilets and a food prep-aration area, as well as bins of rocks to weigh down your tent against the infamous gales.

9 Flora
Look for tiny, hardy flowers contrasting with the dark lava walls near the springs. Pink thrifts, moss campion, purple self-heals **(left)**, aromatic thyme, white cottongrass and violet butterworts are common.

6 Ljótipollur
Don't let the name, Icelandic for "ugly puddle", put you off visiting this lake, an attractive blue pool inside a bright red scoria depression.

7 Hekla
The Hekla volcano **(below)**, towering over southwest Iceland, has been erupting at 10-year intervals *(see p115)*. The road to Landmannalaugar traverses ash dunes and lava fields from the 1970 eruption.

8 Frostastaðavatn
Packed with trout and Arctic char, this lake is a favourite fishing spot. The hike around the shore takes 3 hours and it is a fairly easy walk, except for a stretch over a lava field.

HIKING LAUGAVEGUR

The Laugavegur hike isn't especially difficult but you do need to be self-sufficient and prepared against possible bad conditions. Warm, weatherproof, clothing and hiking boots are necessary, carry maps and a compass, and bring your own food as there are no shops along the way. Bunkhouses must be booked in advance. Campsites are laid out at about 15 km (9 mile) intervals and campers need strong tents in good condition along with cooking gear.

10 Hrafntinnusker
Hrafntinnusker is a huge "reef" made of obsidian (black volcanic glass) located southwest of Landmannalaugar. Look for weathered outcrops around the lava field and on Bláhnúkur, along with smaller pebbles all over.

NEED TO KNOW

MAP D5 ▪ Mid-Jun–mid-Sep: daily buses from Reykjavík and Skaftafell ▪ www.landmannalaugar.info

Open mid-Jun–late Aug

▪ Book bunkhouses at Landmannalaugar and along the Laugavegur hiking trail in advance with the Icelandic Touring Club at *www.fi.is*

▪ The hot springs can get very busy at weekends and when the Reykjavík bus arrives between 1 and 3pm. Time your soak carefully to avoid the crowds.

▪ In July and early August, you can buy burgers, soft drinks and coffee at the Fjallabúð Café, housed in an old bus at the campsite. There are no other places to eat within 50 km (31 miles).

TOP 10 ⭐ Jökulsárlón

Jökulsárlón is a broad lagoon on the southeastern coast, where the nose of the Breiðamerkurjökull glacier edges down to the sea. The lagoon formed after the glacier began receding during the 1940s and today presents a striking scene, filled by a mass of icebergs freshly broken off the glacier. With a deep, black-sand beach behind you and the white mass of Europe's largest icecap, Vatnajökull, on the horizon, Jökulsárlón is a great spot to stretch your legs on the long drive from Vík to Höfn.

The Lagoon ①
Around 5 km (3 miles) across and fairly narrow, this is the deepest lagoon in Iceland **(right)**. By contrast, its outflow, the Jökulsá, is the country's shortest river.

② The Beach
Translucent, weirdly shaped boulders of ice **(below)** – the smaller, depleted remains of Jökulsárlón's icebergs – wash downstream to the sea. There they get stranded on the black-sand beach, making for some evocative photographs.

⑤ Aquatic Life
Jökulsárlón's cool, deep waters attract herring and trout, which in turn make it a good place to see seals – often spotted snoozing on ice floes **(below)**. Porpoises and other small whales also visit on occasion.

③ Icebergs
The pale blue icebergs create a natural sculpture exhibition, constantly changing shape as they melt, breaking into smaller floes. Eventually they are small enough to float to the sea.

④ Vatnajökull
The lagoon is a good spot to get a feel for Vatnajökull's vast size (see pp24–5). Breiðamerkurjökull is 15 km (9 miles) across but even this is only a fraction of the massive white icefield before you.

⑥ Breiðárlón
For similar but more remote scenery, head to Breiðárlón, 6 km (4 miles) west along the highway, then 3 km (2 miles) north on a gravel road.

7 Ice Caves

Formed by meltwater flowing into glaciers through cracks and crevasses, ice caves, also known as crystal caves, can be found in Vatnajokull and Langjokull.

8 Birds

Bird lovers should look out for the ground-nesting Arctic terns **(above)** and the bulkier brown Arctic skuas. Both tend to dive-bomb anything that gets too close to their nests.

BRIDGING THE RIVERS

Bridging the numerous deep, ever-shifting glacial rivers that thread their way seawards all along the south coast was such a massive undertaking that the national highway around the country – the Ringroad – got completed only in 1974. Before this, places like Jökulsárlón were well off the beaten track, as the main road between Skaftafell and Reykjavík was, in reality, just a gravel track.

NEED TO KNOW

MAP G5 ■ Visitor Centre: 478 2222
■ www.vatnajukulsthjodgardur.is
■ www.jokulsarlon.is

Open Apr–Oct; call ahead to book a boat tour as the timings of the tours can vary

■ All buses travelling along the south coast of Iceland stop at Jökulsárlón for around 30 minutes, which is long enough to take in the lagoon and walk down to the sea to look at the ice boulders.

■ The café at the Visitor Centre opens from 9am to 7pm all year round. It serves inexpensive hot food, snacks and coffee. Waffles and seafood soup are specialities here.

9 Visitor Centre

Jökulsárlón's small Visitor Centre **(above)** has a café selling fast food and hot drinks, and a few shelves of souvenir postcards and T-shirts. Climb the black hillock out front for great views of the lagoon.

10 Boat Tour

For a chance to enter the maze of icebergs right up against the glacier snout, take a Zodiac boat tour **(below)** from the Visitor Centre. With a bit of luck, you might also get close to the seals.

The Top 10
of Everything

**The northern lights above houses
on the outskirts of Reykjavík**

⓾ Moments in History

Naddoður discovers Iceland

① AD 860: Viking Exploration

Around this time a Viking named Naddoður discovered an uninhabited coastline to the northwest of the Faroe Islands. This new land was later visited by the Norseman Flóki Vilgerðarson, who, having spent a harsh winter here, gave it the name "Ísland" (Iceland).

② AD 870: Reykjavík Settled

Norwegians Ingólfur Arnarson and Hjörleifur Hróðmarsson set sail for Iceland with their families. Hjörleifur was murdered by his slaves after he settled at Hjörleifshöfði. Ingólfur became Iceland's first permanent settler and built his home-stead at a place he named Reykjavík *(see p76)*.

Statue of Ingólfur Arnarson

③ AD 930: Alþing Established at Þingvellir

All available land in Iceland was settled by AD 930 and regional chieftains found it necessary to form a national government. Rejecting the idea of a king, they opted for a commonwealth. The Parliament (Alþing) was convened annually at Þingvellir, where laws were made and disputes settled.

④ AD 1000: Iceland Becomes Christian

The majority of Iceland's original settlers believed in Norse gods. During the 10th century, however, Norway's king Ólafur Tryggvason threatened Iceland with invasion unless it converted to Christianity. Accordingly, the Alþing of AD 1000 adopted Christianity as Iceland's official religion.

⑤ 1262: The Old Treaty with Norway

During the 13th century, power moved into the hands of wealthy landowners, who plunged the island into civil war. Norway stepped in as peacemaker, and in the year 1262 Iceland accepted Norwegian sovereignty as a semi-independent state under the Old Treaty.

⑥ 1397: Denmark Takes Over

Denmark's ruler, the "Lady King" Margrete, absorbed the Norwegian throne under the Kalmar Union. Later on, Denmark rejected Iceland's claims of autonomy, and in 1661 used military force to impose absolute rule.

⑦ 1550: Iceland Becomes Lutheran

The Danish king appointed Gissur Einarsson as Iceland's first Lutheran bishop in the year 1542. As the nation reluctantly adopted the new faith imposed upon it, Iceland's last Catholic bishop, Jón Arason,

Stained-glass portrait of Jón Arason

took up arms. He was defeated at Skálholt and executed on 7 November 1550.

8 1783: Lakagígar Eruption

A major volcanic eruption along the Laki craters (see p25) flooded south eastern Iceland with lava. Poisonous fallout wiped out agriculture across the land. Famine over the next three years killed one in three Icelanders, and Denmark considered evacuating the entire population to Jutland.

9 1944: Iceland Declares Independence

The mid-19th century saw rising nationalism in Iceland, forcing Denmark to return legislative power to the Alþing in 1874. Nazi Germany's invasion of Denmark during World War II nullified its hold over Iceland, and on 17 June 1944 the country's first president, Sveinn Björnsson, proclaimed Icelandic independence, ending 700 years of foreign rule.

10 2008: Banking Crisis

By the early 2000s, Iceland's agricultural economy had diversified into financial speculation. Icelandic businesses invested in overseas companies, fuelling a credit economy with high interest rates and rapid inflation. When the bubble burst in 2008, the banks collapsed, ruining many and forcing the government to devalue Iceland's currency.

TOP 10 FIGURES IN HISTORY

1 Flóki Vilgerðarson
The Viking who named Iceland and was known as Hrafna-Flóki, or Raven-Flóki, after his pet birds.

2 Ingólfur Arnarson
Iceland's first official settler, who left his native Norway following a feud with the local earl.

3 Leifur Eiríksson
Son of Eirík the Red, Leifur sailed west from Greenland in the year 1000 and discovered America.

4 Guðríður Þorbjarnardóttir
Mother of the first European born in North America, she later made a pilgrimage to Rome.

5 Snorri Sturluson
The 13th-century historian, politician and author of *Egil's Saga* (see p84), the *Heimskringla* and the *Prose Edda*.

6 Jónas Hallgrímsson
Influential Romantic poet who shaped nationalist pride during the 1800s.

7 Jón Sigurðsson
Leader of the independence movement, he promoted the move for Iceland's political autonomy from Denmark.

8 Hannes Hafsteinn
Iceland's first home minister in 1904, who oversaw a period of modern ization and social change.

9 Vigdís Finnbogadóttir
Iceland's first democratically elected female head of state who served as President from 1980 until 1996.

10 Jóhanna Sigurðardóttir
The world's first openly gay political leader, who served as Prime Minister of Iceland from 2009 to 2013.

Former Prime Minister, Jóhanna

TOP10 Churches

1 Dómkirkjan
MAP L2 ■ Austurvöllur Square, Reykjavík ■ 520 9700 ■ Open 10am–4pm Mon–Fri

This small, neoclassical Lutheran cathedral was consecrated in 1796, just as Reykjavík, which was previously just a collection of farm buildings and warehouses, began to coalesce into Iceland's first town. The unadorned interior shows off the building's simple proportions to beautiful effect.

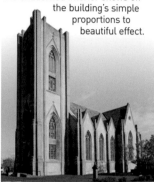

Landakotskirkja cathedral

2 Landakotskirkja
MAP K2 ■ Túngata 13, Reykjavík ■ 552 5388 ■ Open 7:30am–6:30pm daily ■ www. catholica.is

Iceland's Catholic faith was fiercely stomped out in 1550, so it is not surprising that this cathedral dates back to only 1929. Perhaps not to offend Protestant feelings, the building is functional and plain in the extreme and only the entrance and statues of the Virgin Mary, and other saints, give the denomination away.

3 Bænahús
MAP E5 ■ Núpsstaður, near Kirkjubæjarklaustur

Wedged below tall cliffs, Núpsstaður is a collection of antique turf farm buildings, including Bænahús church, which was once considered Iceland's remotest holding despite its proximity to the coast. Until the

Bænahús church, Núpsstaður

1850s the nearest harbours were at distant Eyrarbakki and Djúpivogur, and stock had to be transported inland via the highland roads.

4 Grund
MAP E3 ■ Grund, Eyjafjörður

Most unusually for Iceland, this church has an onion-domed cupola topping its wooden tower and Romanesque mini-spires. Although built in 1905 by trader Magnús Sigurðsson, the building has undergone renovations. There has been a chuch here since the Middle Ages and Grund was once a wealthy holding. The treasures of the church include a 15th-century chalice, kept at the National Museum in Reykjavík.

Grund church

5 Hallgrímskirkja
Vast in scale as it stands proudly over Reykjavík, Hallgrímskirkja is not a cathedral, although it is Iceland's biggest church (see p76). Designed in

Hallgrímskirkja

8 Þingeyrakirkja

This beautiful stone church in northern Iceland stands close to a Viking assembly site and the presumed location of the country's first monastery *(see p98)*. Þingeyrakirkja's medieval alabaster altar was carved in England. The ceiling of the church is painted blue and studded with hundreds of gold stars creating a gorgeous effect.

1945, construction was allegedly undertaken by a family firm of just two people and the building work dragged on, incredibly, until 1986.

6 Hóladómkirkja

MAP D2 ■ Hólar í Hjaltadal
■ 895 9850 ■ Open mid-May–Aug:
10am–6pm daily ■ Regular buses
■ www.kirkjan.is/holadomkirkja

Seat of Iceland's second bishopric since the 12th century, this remote cathedral dates to the 1760s, though some sculptures – and the ornate altarpieces – are centuries older. The country's first printing press was founded here in 1530 by Bishop Jón Arason, who is buried in a small adjacent chapel within the tower.

7 Skálholtskirkja

MAP C5 ■ Skálholt,
Biskupstungur ■ 486 8870 ■ Daily bus
from Selfoss, mid-May–Sep; tours from
Reykjavík ■ Adm ■ www.skalholt.is

Iceland's first bishopric, from 1056 until 1801, Skálholt became an important educational centre and at one point was the country's largest settlement. The memorial outside is dedicated to Iceland's last Catholic bishop, Jón Arason, and the 13th-century tomb is that of Bishop Páll Jónsson. Concerts are also sometimes held at the cathedral.

9 Víðimýri

MAP D3 ■ Víðimýri,
Skagafjörður ■ 453 6173 ■ www.
glaumbaer.is/is/information

The 19th-century tiny turf chapel at Víðimýri is one of only six surviving in Iceland, with an attractive timber interior. Check out the walls, weather-proofed by stacking thick slices of earth in a herringbone pattern, and the pretty summertime flowers growing on the grassy roof.

10 Strandakirkja

MAP C5 ■ Selvogur, near
Þorlákshöfn ■ 483 3797 ■ Open
May–Sep

Standing beyond a small seashore hamlet at the eastern end of the Reykjanes peninsula, Strandakirkja is a picture-perfect 19th-century church, painted pale blue and built on a firm base of square-cut lava blocks. According to local legend, it was funded by a group of grateful sailors who made it ashore at this very spot during a storm.

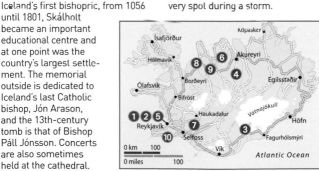

🔟 Museums in Reykjavík

1 Listasafn Íslands National Gallery

A core collection of works by seminal Icelandic artists such as Ásgrímur Jónsson contrasts with avant-garde installations by the likes of Krístján Guðmundsson and Hrafnkell Sigurðsson. The gallery (see p75) also showcases works by big names, including Picasso and Munch. The Vasulka Chamber is dedicated to video and multimedia art .

Exhibit at Þjóðminjasafn Íslands

2 Þjóðminjasafn Íslands National Museum

An exploration of Iceland's history and culture, the permanent exhibition – Making of a Nation – shows how the country took shape. Viking graves, medieval church sculptures and 19th-century clothing, as well as modern-day objects are on display (see p76). There are also regular temporary exhibitions.

3 Reykjavík Art Museum

MAP L2 ▪ Hafnarhús, Tryggvagata 17 ▪ 411 6400 ▪ Open 10am–5pm Fri–Wed, 10am–10pm Thu ▪ Adm (under-18s free); Jun–Aug: free guided tours once a week ▪ www.artmuseum.is

The contemporary branch of the museum's three sites is located by the harbour. As well as hosting a diverse programme of exhibitions, it also houses a collection of paintings by Icelandic artist Erró, born in 1932. Another branch focuses on the work of Jóhannes Kjarval (see p76), and the third centres on Ásmundur Sveinsson.

4 Landnámssýningin Settlement Exhibition

The centrepiece to this excellent subterranean museum (see p75) is the oval foundation wall of a Viking longhouse, with a distinctive underlying layer of volcanic ash, dated AD 871. Holographic dioramas and artifacts, including wooden farm implements and corroded axes, bring it all to life. Look for sacrificial cow bones among the foundations.

5 The Einar Jónsson Sculpture Museum

Einar Jónsson's pieces owe a good deal to the early 20th-century nationalist movements across Europe, with heroic figures in dramatic, iconic arrangements (see p78). One of the

Sculpture by Einar Jónsson

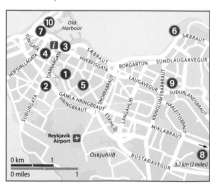

A stone sculpture by Sigurjón Ólafsson

favourites is St George resting on his sword, holding his shield aloft, with the dragon coiling behind.

6 Sigurjón Ólafsson Sculpture Museum

Located along the foreshore, this gallery (see p78) was founded by the artist's widow. It displays Sigurjón's realistic portraits and modernist, abstract works, ranging from smoothly contoured sculptures to giant installations looking like totem poles made out of driftwood, bronze and steel.

7 The Saga Museum

MAP Q5 ▪ Grandagardi 2 ▪ 511 1517 ▪ Open 10am–6pm daily ▪ Adm ▪ www.sagamuseum.is

This hugely enjoyable museum features characters from the Icelandic sagas, including larger-than-life Vikings such as the violent but gifted Egil Skallagrímsson, Leif Eiríksson, discoverer of America, and the ill-fated poet, politician and saga author Snorri Sturluson. There is realistic detail in the clothing and period buildings, as well as the vivid Viking-age noises and smells.

8 Árbæjarsafn

MAP P6 ▪ Kistuhyl 4, Árbær ▪ 411 6300 ▪ Bus 5, 12 or 16 from Hlemmur & 6 or 12 from Lækjartorg ▪ Open Jun–Aug: 10am–5pm daily; Sep–May: 1–5pm daily; guided tours in English at 1pm ▪ Adm ▪ www.reykjavikcitymuseum.is

A former farm has been converted into an open-air museum of old buildings, farm machinery and period artifacts. The best permanent exhibit is the turf-roofed timber house from the late 19th century. Regular events, when the machinery is fired up and domestic animals wander around, bring the place to life.

9 Ásmundur Sveinsson Sculpture Museum

Part of the Reykjavík Art Museum (see p78), this building is an attraction in itself. The real pleasure is walking around the sculpture garden outside, which is full of Ásmundur's depictions of themes from history and folklore, both his early figurative works and his later abstract pieces. Inside are smaller pieces in a variety of media.

10 Vikin Maritime Museum

MAP K1 ▪ Grandagarður 8, 101 Reykjavík ▪ 411 6340 ▪ Open 10am–5pm daily ▪ Adm ▪ www.maritimemuseum.is

This museum at Reykjavík's old harbour tries to convey a flavour of life on the ocean. Pick of the exhibits is the magnificent Óðinn, a coastguard vessel docked at the museum's pier.

Óðinn, Vikin Maritime Museum

🔟 Museums Around Iceland

① Borgarnes Settlement Center

The exhibitions *(see p83)* are in two halves and their entry price includes audio guides (in 15 languages). Upstairs, Iceland's settlement is covered in detail, from its discovery by the Vikings to the establishment of the Alþing in AD 930. Downstairs, *Egil's Saga (see p84)* is brought to life with carvings of key scenes from this violent tale.

Carving of Egil's Saga

② Icelandic Emigration Centre

MAP D2 ▪ Hofsós ▪ 453 7935 ▪ Buses in summer ▪ Open Jun–Sep: 11am–6pm daily; Oct–May: by appointment only ▪ Adm ▪ www.hofsos.is

The lonely setting of this museum on the north coast gives some idea of the feelings endured by the thousands of 19th-century Icelanders who left for Canada following a catastrophic series of harsh winters and volcanic eruptions.

③ Skógar Museum

MAP D6 ▪ Skógar ▪ 487 8845 ▪ Buses from Reykjavík and Höfn ▪ Open Jun–Aug: 9am–6pm daily; Sep–May: 10am–5pm daily ▪ Adm ▪ www.skogasafn.is

The museum's collection documents over 1,000 years of history. It hosts a collection of more than 18,000 regional artifacts exhibited in three spaces: a

Skógar Museum

Folk Museum, Open Air Museum and a Technical Museum. It also houses a souvenir shop and cafeteria.

Herring Era Museum

④ Herring Era Museum

MAP D2 ▪ Snorragata 15, Siglufjörður ▪ 467 1604 ▪ Buses in summer ▪ Open 10am–5pm daily ▪ Adm ▪ www.sild.is

Increasingly popular with tourists today, Siglufjörður was once – until herring stocks collapsed in the 1960s – Iceland's busiest herring port, its harbour crammed with boats. The award-winning museum documents those hectic times in photos, models and dioramas, including photos of the "herring girls" who gutted and salted the catches.

⑤ Orka Náttúrinnar Geothermal Energy Exhibition

MAP C5 ▪ Hellisheiði Power Plant, 20 mins drive from Reykjavík towards Hveragerði on Route 1 ▪ Open 9am–5pm daily ▪ Adm ▪ www.geothermalexhibition.com

The state-of-the-art exhibition shows how geothermal energy is used in Iceland and its potential as a non-polluting, sustainable energy source. The guided tour is excellent and the interactive multimedia exhibits are fascinating as well, especially the earthquake simulator.

6 Westfjords Maritime Museum

Ísafjörður was settled in the 1580s and later became a busy port for saltfish. This museum, overlooked by the mountain of Eyrarfjall, is located in the town's 18th-century Turnhús (the towerhouse which acted as a lookout post), documents those times. Photos reveal that the town centre has changed little since the early 20th century.

7 Icelandic Museum of Rock & Roll

MAP B5 ■ Hjallavegur 2, 260 Reykjanesbær ■ 420 1030 ■ Open 11am–6pm daily ■ Adm (under 16s free) ■ www.rokksafn.is

This museum documents the story of Icelandic rock and pop music, covering the likes of Sigur Rós and Björk. Visitors can borrow iPads so they can listen to featured artists' music and try out instruments in the Sound Lab. A new 12-m (39-ft) interactive wall shows a timeline and history of local artists.

8 Langabúð

MAP G4 ■ Djúpivogur ■ 478 8220 ■ Buses run between Höfn and Egilsstaðir in summer ■ Open Jun–Sep: 10am–6pm daily ■ Adm ■ www.langabud.is

The oldest wooden building on Djúpivogur harbour, Langabúð was built as a warehouse in 1790 and is now a cultural centre, folk museum and memorial to the well-known Icelandic artist Ríkarður Jónsson (1888–1977) who

Húsavík Whale Museum

taught drawing and sculpture. His works are on display here. It also has a coffee shop.

9 Húsavík Whale Museum

Overlooking Húsavík harbour, where whaling boats are now used for whale-watching tours, the Húsavík Whale Museum (see p96) uses videos, relics and skeletons to educate visitors about whales. It is essential viewing before heading seawards to see the whales in the flesh.

10 Viking World

MAP B5 ■ Víkingabraut 1, 260 Reykjanesbær ■ 422 2000 ■ Open 7am–6pm daily ■ Adm ■ www.vikingaheimar.is

The modern, glass-sided museum just outside Keflavík houses the *Íslendingur*, a full-scale reproduction of a wooden Viking longship unearthed in Norway in the 1880s. *Íslendingur* was built by Captain Gunnar Marel Eggertsson, who sailed in it to New York in 2000 to celebrate the millennium of the Viking discovery of North America.

🔟 Waterfalls

Water splashing from under the moss-covered lava bank, Hraunfossar

1 Hraunfossar and Barnafoss
MAP C4

Two adjacent falls *(see p83)*, with very different characters, can be found within easy reach of Borgarnes on the west coast. At Hraunfossar, blue water splashes out from under a lush moss-covered lava bank and gurgles down into the river, while Barnafoss forms a short, savage set of rapids as it cuts through a narrow canyon just upstream.

2 Glymur
MAP C4

Iceland's tallest waterfall, Glymur drops nearly 200 m (658 ft) off the top of a plateau inland from Hvalfjörður, along the west coast. Legend has it that a mythical beast, half-man and half-whale, swam up the waterfall and into Hvalvatn, the lake at the top – where whale bones have indeed been found.

3 Gullfoss

This large, beautiful and always impressive two-tier fall *(see pp18–19)* sits on the Hvítá river around 75 km (47 miles) northeast of Reykjavík. It is one of Iceland's most visited sights, along with nearby Geysir and Þingvellir. In the early 20th century, it was at the heart of the country's first environmental dispute.

4 Seljalandsfoss
MAP D6

Fed by the melting water from Eyjafjallajökull icecap, Seljalandsfoss is narrow and not especially tall, but it drops into a meadow along the south coast with surprising force. Adventurous visitors can take a walk along the path behind the water curtain, for a good soak. Look out for several smaller falls nearby.

5 Dettifoss

Europe's biggest waterfall in terms of volume *(see p25)*, this monster at Jökulsárgljúfur National Park can be heard miles away. The stark setting, where the river drops 45 m (148 ft) between the shattered cliffs of the Jökulsá canyon, adds to the spectacle. Upstream is another waterfall, Selfoss, only 10 m (33 ft) high but 70 m (230 ft) across.

6 Skógafoss
MAP D6

Just walking up along the river to this mighty waterfall is an incredible experience: as you approach, the flat gravel plain vanishes inside soaking clouds of spray and an extraordinary level of noise. Climb a staircase up to the top for more cascades and views out over southern Iceland's coastline.

The cascades of Skógafoss

7 Dynjandi
MAP B2

This waterfall in the Westfjords near Hrafnseyri cascades over several tiers of basalt boulders in a 60-m (198 ft) wide, 100-m (329-ft) drop. Crashing over all those boulders gives Dynjandi ("the Thunderer")

its name, but views seawards over grassy dales make it a beautiful place to camp out.

8 Goðafoss
MAP E2

Located between Akureyri and Mývatn, this "Waterfall of the Gods" *(see p98)* is where the 10th-century Law-speaker Þorgeir Ljósvetningagoði, who championed the introduction of Christianity to Iceland, disposed of the statues of pagan Norse gods in the year 1000. The ice-blue water channels over several falls, with easy walking tracks between them.

9 Ófærufoss
MAP E5

This waterfall *(see p30)* thunders into the Eldgjá canyon on the Fjallabak Route between Landmannalaugar and Skaftafell. The river flows along the top and drops into the canyon, gouging out a broad, scree-ridden pool before falling again as a smaller curtain onto the plain.

10 Aldeyjarfoss
Off the northern end of the rugged Sprengisandur Route across Iceland's Interior, Aldeyjarfoss *(see p117)* cuts a rough scar across the huge Suðurárhraun lava field, exposing layers of ash and rock that have settled over successive eruptions. Although only 20 m (66 ft) high, the falls are very forceful and electrify an otherwise lifeless terrain.

Aldeyjarfoss, at the north end of the Sprengisandur Route

TOP 10 Volcanoes

Ash cloud rising from Eyjafjallajökull

1 Eyjafjallajökull
MAP D6

In March 2010, an eruption of the Eyjafjallajökull volcano began at the Fimmvörðuháls hiking trail *(see p54)*. A month later, as it petered out, a much bigger eruption started in the main crater of the volcano. From the 4th until the 20th of April, a vast cloud of volcanic ash spread across large areas of Europe. Many countries closed their airspace, affecting hundreds of thousands of passengers. The volcano remains active, but it is closely monitored by the country's Meteorological Office.

2 Hekla

This large, lively mountain *(see p31)* has erupted over a dozen times since Iceland was settled, most famously burying a host of nearby Viking farms under ash in 1104. The last major stirrings were in the 1940s, but there have been many smaller incidents since then. In between eruptions, experienced hikers can walk to the top of this mountain.

3 Snæfell
MAP A4

This stratovolcano *(see p104)* – one whose cone has built up gradually over successive eruptions – is believed to have last erupted around AD 250 and today it is covered by the Snæfellsjökull icecap *(see pp26–7)*. Unlike Hekla, whose top is usually shrouded by cloud, Snæfell's bright white peak stands like a beacon over the west coast of the country.

4 Öræfajökull
MAP F5

Iceland's tallest volcano is located near Ingólfshöfði. Its terrible explosion in 1362 buried almost a third of the country under gravel and forced the abandonment of farms all along the south coast. Another eruption in 1727 caused less damage, mainly because only a few people had returned to live here.

Lakagígar, southern Iceland

5 Lakagígar

In 1783, the countryside inland from Kirkjubæjarklaustur split open a huge rent, which belched fire and poisonous fumes for seven months *(see p116)*. It is said that Kirkjubæjarklaustur itself was saved by the actions of pastor Jón Steingrímsson, who bundled the town's population into the church and prayed that they be spared – the lava halted right at the church boundary.

6 Eldfell
MAP C6

The 1973 eruption of Eldfell on Heimaey, in the Westman Islands, buried a third of the town under lava and the rest under ash. But the harbour was saved – and even improved – by the spraying of seawater onto the lava front as it edged down from the volcano.

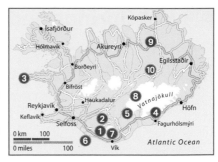

7 Katla
MAP D6

This dangerous volcano lies buried beneath the Mýrdalsjökull icecap near Skógar on the south coast. It erupts on average every 70 years, and the last one, in 1918, sent a titanic flood of meltwater and gravel down nearby valleys. Recent activity in the area, including earthquakes in the caldera, might be signalling the next eruption.

8 Grímsvötn
MAP E4

Currently Iceland's most active volcano, Grímsvötn smoulders away 400 m (1,315 ft) below the massive Vatnajökull ice cap. A massive jökulhlaup – a volcanically induced flash flood – tore out from under the Skeiðarárjökull glacier in 1995, destroying several bridges. There was another eruption in May 2011.

9 Krafla

The Krafla Fires of 1975–84, a striking repetition of the Mývatn Fires of the 1720s *(see p21)*, happened at a bad time: they delayed the completion of the Leirbotn Geothermal Power Station, under construction at the time, for over a decade. However, the new source of natural heat might make it possible to increase the station's projected 60 MW output.

10 Askja

In 1875, a small vent in the Askja *(see p21)* caldera exploded with such force that it vaporized 2 cubic km (1 cubic mile) of rock, burying farms across northeastern Iceland in a thick layer of pumice and sparking mass emigration to Canada. Askja last erupted in 1961, but the current eruption of Bárðabunga at Holuhraun is connected to the system.

Askja, northeastern Iceland

🔟 Hot Springs and Geysers

Geothermal spa water at the Blue Lagoon

1 The Blue Lagoon

Only Icelanders could turn the outflow from a geothermal power station into the country's premier tourist attraction (see pp14–15). The first thing you see when you arrive is people emerging from the milky-blue water with their faces covered in the fine white silt mask that is also sold here as a beauty product.

2 Jarðböðin Nature Baths

This mineral-rich natural spa (see pp20–21) uses its dramatic location on a steaming volcanic ridge overlooking Lake Mývatn to good effect. The water at Myvatn Nature Baths is high in minerals and the steam in the baths is natural, coming up from the earth.

3 Geysir

Now just a flooded crater at the top of a mound, Geysir (see pp16–17) once set the benchmark for erupting hot spouts worldwide (even giving them their name) until its subterranean vents became clogged with debris. A big earthquake in 2008 might have cleared some of them: new bubbling and hissing are the first signs of action for decades.

4 Deildartunguhver
MAP C4

Water emerging at 97°C (207°F) at Deildartunguhver, Europe's largest hot spring, fills the skies with steam near the historic hamlet of Reykholt in the west of Iceland. Since 2017 there have been swish and modern bathing facilities at the site, known as Krauma. There are five geothermal baths, two steam rooms and a relaxation area, as well as an excellent on-site restaurant.

5 Landmannalaugar

Popular with Icelanders and tourists alike, Landmannalaugar (see pp30–31) is the country's finest natural bathing pool – you just can't beat the feeling of soaking away in the hot stream here as a wall of lava towers overhead and fractured orange mountains frame the distance. No other part of the Interior is so wild, yet so accessible.

Jarðböðin Nature Baths

Strokkur erupts

6 Strokkur

Geysir's stand-in, Strokkur (see p16), is a far more reliable successor, erupting 10 times in an hour – even at its peak, Geysir often lay quiet for days at a time. Strokkur is the largest continually active geyser in Iceland (and the one featured in most photographs), reaching impressive heights on a good day.

7 Hengill
MAP R6

This is a popular hiking area west of Hveragerði, with hot springs and steam vents. Many of these springs and vents are being diverted for geothermal energy projects – power plants and miles of silver-coloured pipes for Reykjavík's water and electricity supplies are visible nearby.

8 Námaskarð

This hillside (see p21) to the east of Lake Mývatn, dotted with roaring steam vents and coloured mud pools, does a fantastic job of demonstrating what a raw and powerful force nature can be. The setting, with a lonely, sulphur-rich orange plain stretching away to the south of the hillside, only adds to the impression.

9 Hveravellir

A famous hot spring on the Kjölur (see p115) route across the Interior, this was once used by Eyvindur, the 17th-century outlaw, for warmth and to cook stolen sheep until local farmers chased him out. A great spot to pause during the rough, 5-hour ride from Gullfoss to Akureyri and enjoy a soak in the cooler spa pool alongside the hot spring.

Seltún, on the Reykjanes peninsula

10 Seltún

Down on the Reykjanes peninsula near Reykjavík, there was a decent geyser at Seltún (see p15) in Krýsuvík, until the entire spring exploded in 1999, leaving behind a grey, bubbling pool. But smaller hot springs still seep out of the hills above, making for an interesting half-hour walk – do not leave the marked paths.

0 km   100

0 miles   100

🔟 Places to See Birds and Wildlife

① Lake Mývatn
The country's top venue for viewing wildlife, Lake Mývatn *(see pp20–21)* slots easily into a trip to visit Iceland's laid-back northern capital, Akureyri, and a whale-watching expedition from Húsavík. Ducks and other wildfowl are the main draws, but the elusive Arctic fox and gyrfalcon are also regularly encountered.

② Látrabjarg
Way out in the Westfjords, a trip to Látrabjarg *(see pp28–9)* takes a little bit of planning but you will not forget your first sight of these cliffs, covered by enormous, noisy colonies of nesting seabirds. Stop along the way for a walk or sunbathe on Breiðavík beach.

Hornbjarg, on isolated Hornstrandir

③ Hornbjarg
MAP B1

At 533 m (1,749 ft), Hornbjarg is the highest clifftop on the isolated, completely uninhabited Hornstrandir peninsula, on the Westfjords' extreme northwest. Like Látrabjarg, it is teeming with fulmars, kittiwakes, razorbills and guillemots. There are regular guided day tours, as well as other scheduled boat trips, from Ísafjörður.

④ Dyrhólaey
MAP D6 ■ Closed 7pm–9am

The headland of Dyrhólaey is an easy detour off the highway between Skógar and Vík (there are restrictions on cars but it is open for hiking). Apart from puffins and other seabirds, come here to view the black, volcanic-sand beaches and the huge sea arch, which is large enough for a ship to sail through.

Skua, Dyrhólaey

⑤ Jökulsárlón
One of the most spellbinding sights of southeastern Iceland, this deep, iceberg-filled lagoon *(see pp32–3)* between the sea and Breiðamerkurjökull glacier is a great place to spot seals and orca, if you are lucky. The sandy plains on either side are full of nesting terns and skuas – and arctic foxes looking for a meal.

⑥ Skjálfandi
MAP E2

A summer sailing trip out from Húsavík to Skjálfandi, the broad bay offshore, is certain to put you within viewing range of marine mammals. You are most likely to see seals and dolphins but with any luck you will also encounter spectacular humpback whales leaping out of the water.

Humpback whale at Skjálfandi

7 Breiðafjörður
MAP B3

The waters off the west coast are dotted with hundreds of islets and skerries inhabited by thousands of puffins, shags, cormorants and other seabirds. White-tailed sea eagles, one of Iceland's rarest, most majestic species, are also seen here.

8 Garðskagi
MAP B5

Close to Keflavík International Airport, this little tongue of land overlooks a gravelly beach where you can easily spot redshanks, sanderlings, turnstones, eider duck and other shorebirds – look out to sea for gannets.

The striped red lighthouse was once used to monitor bird migration.

Garðskagi lighthouse

9 Ingólfshöfði
MAP F5 ■ Hiking tours: mid-May–Aug: Mon–Sat at 10:15am & 1:30pm; tractor from Ingólfshöfði car park ■ www.puffintour.is ■ Adm

In AD 874, Ingólfur Arnarson – Iceland's first settler – landed his ship on this cape, located halfway between Skaftafell and Jökulsárlón. Puffins, great skua and other birds nest here in the summer.

10 Jökulsá á Dal
MAP G3

With river systems and integrated wetlands merging from the highland moors around Snæfell down to the East Fjords coast, this is a summer breeding ground for geese, swans and all manner of wildfowl. Keep an eye open for reindeer herds too.

TOP 10 ICELANDIC BIRDS

A snow-white ptarmigan

1 Ptarmigan
Grouse renowned for its unique, snow-white winter plumage. A popular Christmas dish in Iceland.

2 Puffin
This charismatic bird nests in burrows on grassy sea cliffs around Iceland between May and September.

3 Arctic Tern
A small, graceful seabird that fearlessly dive-bombs anything that gets too close to its nest.

4 Gyrfalcon
A rare, grey-white falcon that once featured on Iceland's coat of arms. Seek it out around Mývatn Lake.

5 Golden Plover
Common grassland bird whose piping call is eagerly awaited by Icelanders as heralding the spring.

6 Raven
Huge black crow with a harsh call and acrobatic flight, considered highly intelligent by many Icelanders.

7 Meadow Pipit
The island's most abundant bird is a sweet songster, though it can be surprisingly hard to see.

8 White-tailed Sea Eagle
Once persecuted by farmers as a pest, around 80 white-tailed sea eagles now breed in the northwest.

9 Eider Duck
Pied sea duck known for its soft, warm down. It is common around the coast and on lakes inland.

10 Harlequin Duck
This sea duck has an unmistakable blue and red plumage. It breeds inland from May until July around fast-flowing streams.

🔟 Outdoor Activities

Hikers on the Laugavegur trail

1 Hiking
Hiking organizations:
www.fi.is; www.utivist.is; www.mountainguides.is

Nothing gets you closer to Iceland's raw, natural landscape than hiking across it, following established trails ranging in length from an hour to a week. The pick of these are at Landmannalaugar, Jökulsárgljúfur, Skaftafell and Þórsmörk, where you can navigate grassy meadows with wildflowers, lava fields, black-sand deserts and icefields.

2 Swimming
Just about every Icelandic town has an outdoor geothermal swimming pool heated to 28°C (82°F), always with accompanying "hot pot" tubs at 34–38°C (93–100°F), and sometimes with saunas and water slides.

3 River Rafting
www.arcticrafting.is

What Iceland's rivers may lack in size they more than make up for in drama. They tear through narrow volcanic gorges, forming lively rapids. The third longest river in Iceland, the Hvítá is accessible for white-water rafting. The expeditions begin a little distance from Gullfoss waterfall.

4 Fishing
www.icelandangling.com

Recreational deep-sea angling is in its infancy here and most people fly-fish for trout, salmon or char. A permit is essential: those for trout and char are fairly easy to pick up on the spot, but for salmon you need to apply in advance.

5 Snowmobiling
www.glacierjeeps.is

Snowmobiling or Skidooing is an expensive but exhilarating way to tear across snowfields and glaciers at 40 kmph (25 mph). The best place to try it is at Skálafellsjökull, an outrunner of Vatnajökull.

6 Horse Riding
Riding centres: www.eldhestar.is; www.ishestar.is

Iceland's specific breed of horses arrived with the Vikings. Though lacking the size and speed of Arab horses, some have a unique gliding gait, called the *tölt*, which is used for moving softly over the rough Icelandic terrain. Many riding schools and farms offer excursions.

7 Jeep Touring
www.glacierjeeps.is

The harsh Interior – a spread of rough lava fields, gigantic icecaps and gravel plains braided by glacial rivers – is navigable only by high-clearance 4WDs (four-wheel drives). Public buses fit the bill and many operators offer tours in off-road Jeeps.

Jeep wading through the river

8 Skiing and Snowboarding

www.skidasvaedi.is

There are established winter skiing and snowboarding venues around Reykjavík, Akureyri, Hlíðarfjall and in the Westfjords, complete with bunkhouses, ski lifts and graded runs. The most accessible are Bláfjöll, outside Reykjavík, and the popular summer slopes in the west of Snæfellsjökull, with winter cross-country opportunities around Mývatn.

Iceland offers many skiing venues

9 Scuba Diving

MAP C5 ■ www.dive.is; www.diveiceland.com

There are several areas to scuba dive in Iceland – the most popular are Silfra and other spots around Þingvallavatn. With crystal-clear, pale blue water and submerged lava formations, Silfra is rated as one of the best freshwater sites in the world.

10 Aurora Borealis Watching

The northern lights, or aurora borealis, are solar particles fluorescing as they stream across the upper atmosphere, appearing as luminous curtains of colour. They are best viewed on cold nights in years of heavy solar activity, away from sources of light pollution. Ideal conditions occur between November and February.

TOP 10 PLACES TO BATHE AND SWIM

Bathing in the Blue Lagoon

1 The Blue Lagoon
Surreal blue water, steam and black lava boulders feature at this ultimate bathing hotspot (see pp14–15).

2 Laugardalur
Reykjavík's best public pool, complete with a separate children's play pool and a steam room (see p77).

3 Borgarnes
MAP B4 ■ Open 7am–9pm Mon–Fri, 9am–6pm Sat & Sun ■ Adm
The town's swimming pool has exceptional views from the water.

4 Landmannalaugar
Natural hot springs surrounded by lava walls and orange and grey rhyolite mountains (see pp30–31).

5 Jarðböðin
Mývatn's answer to the Blue Lagoon, set up on a hillside among live volcanic scenery (see p21).

6 Selárdalslaug
MAP G2 ■ Open 10am–10pm daily
Tiny public pool near Vopnafjörður, beside the fast-flowing green waters of the Selá river.

7 Krossneslaug
Unforgettable hot springs and a bathing pool in the north, near Norðurfjörður (see p91).

8 Hofsós
The waterline of this seaside pool (see p98) appears to merge with the ocean.

9 Grettislaug
Remote natural hot tub in the northwest, which was the bathing place of Viking outlaw Grettir (see p95).

10 Laugarvatn
MAP C5 ■ Open 10am–9pm Mon–Fri, 10am–6pm Sat & Sun ■ Adm
Huge outdoor pool at the National School for Sports near Geysir.

📶 Hiking Trails

View along the coastal trail from Arnarstapi to Hellnar

1 Arnarstapi to Hellnar
MAP A4

This short coastal walk between the two small villages offers great seascapes and views of Snæfellsjökull's white cone (see p26). Along the way look out for the statue of Bárður Snæfellsás and nesting Arctic terns.

2 Esja
MAP Q5

Esja's 914-m- (2,999-ft-) high plateau rises unmistakably above the bay north of Reykjavík. Its snow-streaked slopes appear to mutate with the changing light – the colours shift from deep brown to pale blue. A return hike from the Mógilsá forestry station takes about 4 hours.

3 Fimmvörðuháls
MAP D6 ■ Summer buses to Skógar and Þórsmörk ■ Trail open mid-Jun–Sep ■ www.fi.is

An overnight trek from Skógar to Þórsmörk (see p26) can be done separately or as an extension

Start of Fimmvörðuháls trail, Skógar

to the Laugavegur trail. From Skógar, climb the steps to the top of the waterfall and follow the river upstream to cross the pass between the Eyjafjallajökull (see p46) and Mýrdalsjökull icecaps, before descending to Þórsmörk.

4 Þingvellir

The mossy valley floor of Þingvellir (see pp12–13) is criss-crossed by easy hiking trails of 1 to 3 hours in duration. Stick to the marked paths, as the vegetated lava flows conceal deep fissures. There are good views along the valley from beside the abandoned farm buildings at Skógarkot.

5 Svartifoss

Skaftafell's most beautiful feature, Svartifoss ("Black Falls"), is located on an easy hiking trail atop Skaftafell plateau (see p25). From the car park near Bölti guesthouse follow the signposts for 10 minutes to the falls that drop into a stunning 30-m- (98-ft-) deep gully.

6 Ásbyrgi

The top of this huge, curved cliff face (see p24) makes an excellent vantage point from which to admire the north of Jökulsárgljúfur National Park. From the park headquarters, follow the footpaths for 5 km (3 miles) through woodland to the top of Ásbyrgi.

7 Heiðmörk Park
MAP Q6

A 28-sq-km (11-sq-mile) spread of lava, woodlands and picnic sites on the edge of Reykjavík city, with easy walking paths looping through it. Extend an excursion here by making a 3-hour circuit of the adjacent lake, Elliðavatn, to view a variety of Iceland's flora.

8 Hveragerði

The steamy hills and valleys immediately north of Hveragerði (see p112) make for a good half-day hike from town, with hot springs along the way (so bring a towel). There is a marked path but be prepared for boggy ground, a couple of river crossings and unpredictable boiling vents.

Steaming vent, Hveragerði

9 Laugavegur

This stunning 4-day hike (see p30) runs from Landmannalaugar, past hot springs and obsidian massifs, to the snowbound Hrafntinnusker plateau, then descends steeply to the green valley around Álftavatn. After passing many glacial rivers, a grey gravel desert at the foot of the Mýrdalsjökull icecap and canyons along Markarfljót, the trail ends in the woodland of Þórsmörk.

10 Þórsmörk

This beautiful highland valley (see p116), with a braided glacial river, is overlooked by Mýrdalsjökull. Carry a map, as few of the many day trails are marked. There are plenty of self-catering cabins and campsites, and daily buses in summer.

TOP 10 ICELANDIC WILD FLOWERS

The vibrant moss campion

1 Moss Campion (Lambagras)
Spongy clumps of this bright pink or purple flower brighten up the muddy, shaley slopes.

2 Mountain Avens (Holtasóley)
Iceland's national flower, whose small fleshy leaves and yellow-centred white petals stand about 7 cm (3 in) high.

3 Arctic River Beauty (Eyrarrós)
Late-flowering plant with distinctive symmetrical, pointed red petals and long leaves.

4 Wild Pansy (Þrenningarfjóla)
Beautiful little plant with violet and yellow petals, which is common locally and abundant in June.

5 Bladder Campion (Holurt)
This white flower is found in small spreads, and has a lilac-pink sac behind the petals.

6 Wild Thyme (Blóðberg)
Tiny, ground-hugging plant with deep red or purple flowers and distinct thyme scent.

7 Wood Cranesbill (Blágresi)
Widespread plant with geranium-like leaves and purple, five-petal flowers; favours woodland edges and reaches 30 cm (12 in) or more.

8 Butterwort (Lyfjagras)
Small, solitary plant with hanging blue flowers and cross-shaped leaves at ground level.

9 Northern Green Orchid (Friggjargras)
Easily missed in the grass, but look for pointed leaves and little white flowers.

10 Purple Saxifrage (Vetrarblóm)
This widespread, but very early-flowering, ground-hugging plant has little pink blooms.

Following pages Interior of Harpa, Reykjavík's Concert Hall and Conference Centre

🔟 Children's Activities

One of many heated outdoor pools

1 Go Swimming

Swimming pools are great places for children to burn off any excess energy, especially after a long car journey. Just about every town in Iceland has a heated pool, which makes it an easy option. Though most of the pools are outdoors, they are especially fun in winter, when snow is falling.

2 Feed the Birds at Tjörnin

In Reykjavík, pick up birdseeds or grains and head to Tjörnin lake (see p78) in the centre of the city to feed whooper swans, greylag geese, eider ducks and mallards. In June and July there are a lot of cute ducklings around too, but note that it is forbidden to feed the birds between May and September.

Whooper swans at Tjörnin

3 Visit the Museums

Iceland's most engaging museums for children are the open-air Árbæjarsafn museum (see p41) of traditional farm life; the Saga Centre at Hvolsvöllur (see p112), which is full of swords and dioramas; Borgarnes Settlement Center (see p42), showcasing spooky recreations of Egil's Saga (see p84); and Húsavík Whale Museum (see p43), with its fascinating skeletons and marine mammal displays.

4 Eat a Hot Dog
MAP L2 ■ Tryggvagata, 101 Reykjavík

Eating a *pylsur* (hot dog) from the flagship Bæjarins Beztu in central Reykjavík (there are four further stands around the city) is a rite of passage for young Icelanders, who form long queues outside this unpretentious mobile stand. Why? The hot dogs taste great – though you might want to hold the onions.

5 Visit Reykjavík Harbour
MAP K1

Reykjavík has a busy harbour, with all types of colourful fishing boats and trawlers sailing in and out on a daily basis or hauled up on slipways for repairs. Look in the waters and you might also see jellyfish. Grab a snack along nearby Geirsgata at either Sægreifinn (see p65), or at Icelandic Fish & Chips (see p65) on Tryggvagata.

6 Go Horse Riding

Short and stocky Icelandic horses are even-tempered, making them child-friendly and a good choice for first-timers. Most of the riding schools cater to children with their flexible schedules and duration of rides (see p52).

7 Picnic at Reykjavík Botanic Gardens

The botanical gardens (see p77) make for a pleasant place for a family outing and picnic, just a short way from downtown Reykjavík. There is plenty of soft grass, ducks and geese wandering about, and – in the summertime at least – beds of colourful endemic flowers. Don't miss the small zoo, which is full of native mammals and birds.

8 Enjoy Whale-Watching

In Iceland there is quite a good chance of seeing minke and humpback whales, orca, sperm whales and even exciting rarities like blue whales. Húsavík (see p96) is the best place to go whale-watching.

9 Hunt for Trolls

Trolls, the frightening, mischief-making giants, are said in local folklore to inhabit several places in Iceland. They turn to stone if they are caught in the sunlight but their oddly shaped, petrified forms can be seen (if you look hard enough) in many lava fields, mountain outcrops and sea stacks.

A rusted shipwreck in Reykjanes

10 Go Beachcombing

Icelandic beaches are full of interesting flotsam and jetsam, from bird feathers and oddly-shaped pebbles to rusted relics from ship-wrecks, tree trunks (which have floated here from Siberia) and even – if you are really lucky – whale bones.

TOP 10 ICELANDIC FOLKTALES

Statue of Sæmundur the Wise

1 Sæmundur the Wise
Founder of an 11th-century ecclesiastical school, who frequently took on and always defeated the Devil.

2 Viking Treasure at Skógafoss
Legend has it that a Viking named Þrasi Þórólfsson hid his hoarded gold in a cave behind the Skógafoss waterfall (see p45).

3 The Beast of Hvalfjörður
This evil, red headed whale terrorized Iceland's west coast until it was lured into a trap.

4 Ormurinn, the Lagarfljót Serpent
Iceland's elusive version of the Loch Ness Monster is said to inhabit Lögurinn lake near Egilsstaðir in the east of the country.

5 Bergþór
A friendly giant who lived at Bláfell, near Geysir, and died around 1000.

6 The Lovestruck Shepherd
A favourite tale about a young man who waded across the Hvítá river to propose to a shepherdess.

7 Eyvindur and Halla
Iceland's most famous medieval outlaw, along with his wife, Halla, survived 20 years on the run.

8 The Origin of Oxará Falls
The falls are said to have been created around AD 930 when the Öxará river at Þingvellir was diverted.

9 Were-Seals
Seals are thought to sometimes adopt human form, especially those that swim close to shore.

10 Snorri
The wily thief Snorri escaped pursuit inside a small cave at Þórsmörk – it is near the bus stop.

🔟 Nightlife

Austur

1 Austur
MAP L2 ■ Austurstræti 7, 101 Reykjavík ■ 568 1907 ■ Open 8pm–1am Thu, 8pm–4:30am Fri & Sat

This club is popular among locals. It boasts a trendy clientele, including celebrities and media people. Live DJs play long into the night and keep the dance floor busy. There's also an extensive menu of wines, cocktails, beers and shots available at the bar.

2 B5
MAP L2 ■ Bankastræti 5, 101 Reykjavík ■ 552 9600 ■ Open 11am–midnight Sun–Wed, 10:30am–1am Thu, 10:30am–2am Fri & Sat

A multifunctional venue, B5 is a burger joint by day, which transforms into a live-music venue on Thursday nights and a nightclub on Fridays and Saturdays. It also has two private lounges (one built in an old bank vault) available for hire.

3 Lebowski Bar
MAP M2 ■ Laugavegur 20a, 101 Reykjavík ■ 552 2300 ■ Open 11–1am Sun–Thu (until 4:30am Fri & Sat) ■ www.lebowskibar.is

Fans of the movie *The Big Lebowski* will appreciate this quirky bowling-themed bar, with its delicious burgers and 24 variations on the White Russian cocktail. Play "spin the wheel" for free drinks. A movie-themed quiz is held every Thursday (from 9pm) and DJs play at weekends.

White Russian cocktail

4 Micro Bar
MAP L2 ■ Vesturgata 2, 101 Reykjavík ■ 847 9084 ■ Open 4pm–midnight daily

Choose from 250 different craft beers, ales, stouts and lagers, including brews you won't find anywhere else in Iceland, at this modern bar. It's run by the folks behind the Gæðingur microbrewery, which is found in the north of the country, so expect to find its beers on tap.

Micro Bar, Reykjavík

5 Bjarni Fel
MAP L2 ■ Austurstræti 20, 101 Reykjavík ■ 561 2240 ■ Open noon–1am Sun–Thu (until 4:30am Fri & Sat)

Locals love this sports bar, named after Icelandic football legend, and sports commentator, Bjarni Felixson. Enjoy watching major sporting events on multiple TV screens as you sample a good selection of pub food and cold beer. Happy hour runs from 9pm to 11pm, when two drinks are sold for the price of one.

6 Prikið
A 50s-style diner, as well as a nightclub, Prikið offers classics such as milkshakes, American pancakes and burgers, including a vegan version. During the day it is the perfect spot for people-watching thanks to its location on the city's main shopping thoroughfare,

while at night it transforms into a lively and fun hip-hop hang-out with DJs, live music and a packed dance floor (see p80).

7 Kaldi
MAP M3
■ Laugavegur 20b, 101 Reykjavík ■ 581 2200 ■ Open noon–1am Sun–Thu, noon–3am Fri & Sat

Convivial café by day and hip craft beer bar by night, this busy spot is an offshoot of the local Kaldi brewery, which has become well-known for its Czech-style beers. As well as its own brews, visitors can enjoy international artisan beers, soft drinks and a limited food menu, whilst relaxing on comfy sofas.

8 Paloma
MAP L2 ■ Naustin 1–3, 101 Reykjavík ■ Open 8pm–1am Sun–Thu, 8pm–4:30am Fri & Sat

Don't be fooled by Paloma's size, which belies the several venues housed within the same building. The Dubliner is a cosy, "Viking-style" pub, with exposed wooden beams and a bar shaped like a longboat. The upstairs club space plays house and electro, whilst the basement's bar has a college party vibe where you can play drinking games. The barman will take your requests for songs.

9 Slippbarinn
MAP K1 ■ Mýrargata 2, 101 Reykjavík ■ 560 8080 ■ Open 11:30am–midnight Sun–Wed (1am Thu–Sat) ■ www.slippbarinn.is

The impressive cocktail menu offered at this bar changes regularly, but the harbour views remain con-sistently inspiring. Located in the Icelandair Hotel Reykjavík Marina, Slippbarinn hosts Icelandic live music, as well as art shows and "pop-up" events of all sorts. Brunch is served at weekends and happy hour is from 3 to 6pm every day.

10 Kaffibarinn
MAP L3 ■ Bergstaðastræti 1, 101 Reykjavík ■ 551 1588 ■ Open 3pm–1am Mon–Fri, 3pm–4:30am Sat & Sun ■ www.kaffibarinn.is

The red corrugated iron exterior, just off Reykjavík's main shopping area, conceals Kaffibarinn's dark interior, with its table-top candles and arty magazines. A trendy and popular place to meet for the first beer of the evening, there are DJs at weekends and, on occasion, live bands.

Kaffibarinn's distinctive exterior

🔟 Fine Dining Restaurants

1 Grillið
Beautifully-furnished and elegant, Grillið is a rooftop restaurant *(see p81)* situated on the eighth floor of the Radisson Hotel. It offers some of the best food in Reykjavík. Select a dish from their four- or seven-course set menus, along with wine or non-alcoholic juice pairings. Enjoy the splendid views of the cityscape from its rooftop.

2 Pakkhús
Located in the little harbour town of Höfn, which is famous for its fresh seafood (especially lobster), this excellent restaurant *(see p105)* is housed in an old wooden warehouse down by the water. It provides an atmospheric setting for visitors to enjoy their meal. Don't miss out on their signature dish – the oven-grilled langoustine. They don't have a booking system, so try to get in early.

3 Rub23
With decent steak and good seafood on offer, Rub23 *(see p81)* is also best visited for some of the freshest sushi you'll probably ever eat. Some of their notable dishes are the delicious tempura lobster, surimi crab and Arctic char nori maki. They offer a takeaway service as well.

Stylish and innovative Vox

4 VOX
With classy interiors, this gourmet restaurant *(see p81)* heads the trend for fresh Icelandic ingredients. The menu offers delicious seafood straight off the trawlers as well as game from specialist farms.

5 Grillmarkaðurinn
The award-winning chefs here *(see p81)* work closely with organic farmers and producers, which is why the dishes are always fresh, seasonal and delicious. Try the salted cod with apple purée and a langoustine salad. They also serve up a good beef tenderloin.

6 Holt Restaurant
Housed inside Hotel Holt, this warm and intimate restaurant *(see p81)* is headed by well-known chef Ragnar Eiríksson. Their menu offers modern European cuisine with Icelandic twists. Order the signature dish here – Arctic char, served with avocado, buttermilk and horseradish. The service here is as elegant as the carefully selected international wine list.

7 Tjöruhúsið
There's something extremely Viking about this long, low barn of a place on Ísafjörður's waterfront *(see p93)*, with diners crowded together

Appetizing dish at Rub23

on wooden benches, but there is nothing at all rough about its seafood. The rich, creamy soups will warm you through on a cold day, and the portions of pan-fried fish are generous. For seafood dishes they usually serve the catch-of-the-day.

8 Fiskmarkaðurinn

Translated as "The Fish Market" Fiskmarkaðurinn is a Nordic restaurant *(see p81)* that has been influenced by Japanese cuisine. Their produce is sourced locally. The sushi on offer is out-standing and the tasting menu is great value for money.

A cod dish at Fiskmarkaðurinn

9 Sjávargrillið

To savour excellent seafood right in the city centre, try this cosy candlelit restaurant *(see p81)*. They offer a wide variety of set menus that feature traditional Icelandic specialities such as pan-fried salted cod, couscous and skyr. A range of set menus are also available.

10 Fjöruborðið

Famed for its langoustine soups and dishes, this restaurant *(see p113)* is housed in an old timber building in Stokkseyri, which is a 45-minute drive from Reykjavík. Their menu and prices change regularly, and so do the opening hours. It is best to check their website or call for up-to-date information. Book in advance.

TOP 10 ICELANDIC FOODS

Roasted Arctic Char

1 Arctic Char
Freshwater fish with a beautifully subtle flavour. The best come from Þingvallavatn and Mývatn.

2 Lobster/langoustine
Superb and plentiful, best served as tails with butter and, perhaps, a little garlic seasoning or cream.

3 Salmon
Wild-caught Atlantic salmon is firm and rich. It is usually eaten smoked or marinated with herbs and served as butter-soft gravlax.

4 Caviar
Iceland's supplies come from capelin and lumpfish, not the classic sturgeon, but are just as delicious.

5 Cod
Most often snacked on as dried, chewy *harðfiskur*, but also cooked fresh and used in soups.

6 Hákarl
Greenland shark, fermented in sand for 6 months to break down toxins. Eye-wateringly strong.

7 Brennivín
Icelandic vodka, flavoured with caraway seeds and affectionately known as "Black Death". Use sparingly.

8 Skyr
Similar to set yoghurt, available in any supermarket in a range of flavours.

9 Lamb
This is the mainstay of Icelandic cuisine. Lamb is eaten fresh, smoked, turned into sausages, or preserved in whey after pressing.

10 Ptarmigan
Plump, partridge-like bird which takes the place of turkey in traditional Christmas meals in Iceland.

🔟 Cheaper Eats in Reykjavík

① Bæjarins Beztu Pylsur
MAP L2 ■ Tryggvagata
■ www.bbp.is ■ Ⓚ

This Reykjavík institution has been popular with locals since 1937. The stand can be found down near the waterfront and its *pylsur* (hot dogs) are a must for visitors to the city. Your money buys you a traditional hot dog, topped with crispy fried onions, ketchup, mustard and a squirt of remoulade sauce.

② Café Garðurinn
MAP M2 ■ Klapparstígur 37
■ 561 2345 ■ Closed D & Sun
■ www.kaffigardurinn.is ■ Ⓚ

This small vegetarian café has a set menu that changes weekly. Flavour combinations are inventive and delicious. They offer a range of crepes, flans, stews and pastas, but tasty soups (served with bread) and quiches are their forte. The "dish of the day" is always excellent value. They serve great coffee and cakes too so be sure to stop by for an afternoon snack.

③ Jómfrúin
MAP L2 ■ Lækjargata 4 ■ 551 0100 ■ www.jomfruin.is ■ Ⓚ

Calling this place a Danish sandwich shop does not do it justice: a good

Jómfrúin, Reykjavík

smørrebrød (open sandwich) involves a choice of prawns, herring, smoked lamb, cheese and countless other ingredients, served on a thick slice of heavy rye bread, and Jómfrúin delivers in style. Be sure to include the fried plaice in your selection of *smørrebrød* toppings.

④ Icelandic Fish & Chips
MAP K2 ■ Tryggvagata 11
■ 511 1118 ■ www.fishandchips.is
■ Ⓚ

Up at Reykjavík's old harbour, this tidy organic bistro delivers just what its name suggests. Choose from the catch-of-the-day or the fresh *skyronaisse* (skyr with fresh herbs or garlic) which is served with sides such as local oven-roasted potatoes and oven-grilled chips. Gluten-free options are also available.

Interiors of Icelandic Fish & Chips

5 Lobster Hut
MAP L2 ■ **Corner of Hverfisgata and Lækjargata** ■ **772 1709** ■ **Closed L & during bad weather** ■ Ⓚ Ⓚ

One of few options on Reykjavík's street food scene, this food truck serves local *humarsúpa* (lobster soup) and lobster sandwiches. Icelandic "lobster" is langoustine, a smaller crustacean whose flavour is extremely close to that of its larger cousin, the rock lobster. The hut's generous portions are grilled fresh to order.

6 Tommi's Burger Joint
MAP P5 ■ **Geirsgata1** ■ **511 0800** ■ Ⓚ

Opened in 1981, this diner-style joint serves up some of the best burgers in town, with good quality patties and freshly baked buns. The reputation of the Joint has spread since Tómas Andrés Tómasson – or Tommi – first started selling burgers and there are now branches in Berlin, London and Copenhagen. The millshakes are a must-try here.

7 Krúa Thai
MAP M3 ■ **Skólavörðustíg 21a** ■ **561 0833** ■ **Closed Sun L** ■ **www.kruathai.is** ■ Ⓚ

One of the few places left in Iceland where you can get an economical restaurant meal – even if it's only a single course. All the old favourites from Thailand, from panang curry to *tom kha gai*, are served in a relaxed, fast-food ambience. The three-course set menu, which is available at lunchtime on weekdays, is excellent value and the beer is inexpensive. Limited takeaway options can also be delivered.

8 Saegreifinn (Sea Baron)
MAP K1 ■ **Geirsgata 8** ■ **553 1500** ■ **www.saegreifinn.is** ■ Ⓚ

A well-known seafood shack by the harbour, this restaurant has a simple yet charming wood-panelled room

dotted with nautical paraphernalia. The menu offers excellent seafood dishes such as silky lobster soup. Vegetable skewers and Skyr desserts are also served here.

9 Þrír Frakkar
MAP L3 ■ **Baldursgata 14** ■ **552 3939** ■ **Closed Sat & Sun L** ■ **www.3frakkar.com** ■ Ⓚ Ⓚ

Set in a charming building in a quiet residential area, the "Three Overcoats" specializes in seafood, with excellent trout, lobster and soups served with a French–Asian twist. The whale steak, pan-fried guillemot breast, smoked puffin and horse tenderloin are cooked in the traditional Icelandic style. Don't miss out on their hashed fish with black bread.

Pan-fried salted cod, Þrír Frakkar

10 Noodle Station
MAP N3 ■ **Laugavegur 103** ■ **551 3198** ■ **www.noodlestation.is** ■ Ⓚ

This cheap and cheerful Asian eatery offers three types of noodle soup – beef, chicken or vegetarian – all made from the Thai owner's grandmother's recipe. Grab a seat if you're lucky or order yours to take away.

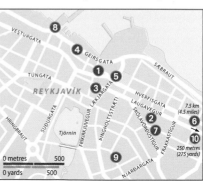

For a key to restaurant price ranges see p81

TOP10 Iceland for Free

The spectacular aurora borealis

1 Aurora Borealis

Extremely low light pollution in its night skies makes Iceland a superlative place to see the dancing curtains of the northern lights *(see p53)*. Come in winter (they do not appear on short summer nights) during years in which there is increased solar activity. For the best views get away from Reykjavík.

2 Camping

While it is possible to camp anywhere for free outside of the city boundaries or national parks, visitors are encouraged by the Environment Agency of Iceland *(see p127)* to opt for organized campsites. Always ask for permission from local landowners, as they can suggest the best places to pitch a tent away from livestock or crops. Leave things as you find them, taking your rubbish away with you.

3 Berjamór

Join Icelanders in picking wild crowberries (similar to blueberries) from late summer to early autumn. They grow all over the place, but ask around to find the best spots. Don't be greedy: leave some for the birds, who need them to get through the harsh winters.

4 Natural Thermal Pools

Since Viking times, hot springs have been channelled into fabulous natural spas. The pick of the bunch is at Landmannalaugar *(see pp30–31)*, but others include Seljavallalaug *(see p112)* near Skógar, right below the site of the 2010 eruption that closed down European airspace. The visitors are expected to follow strict guidelines on personal hygiene.

Thermal pool at Landmannalaugar

5 Hiking

There are several adventurous hikes within an hour's drive of Reykjavík. The closest is Esja *(see p54)*, which offers remarkable views over the city from its summit. Other trails include a trek up to Glymur *(see p44)* – one of the highest waterfalls in Iceland – and Reykjadalur, which is a hot spring set in a valley.

6 Wildlife Watching

Iceland is a great place to spy on wildlife. You will find seals and tee-ming seabird colonies all around the coast (especially at Vík, Látrabjarg and the Westman Islands), reindeer herds in the eastern highlands, shy Arctic foxes everywhere, and rare ducks and other waterfowl at Mývatn lake.

7 Þingvellir Parliament Site

MAP C5

Even if it weren't intimately linked to key events in Icelandic history, Þingvellir (see pp12–13) would still be a spectacular place: a broad rift valley sided in basalt columns where the Eurasian and American contin-ental plates are visibly tearing apart. There's some good hiking here too.

8 Scale Model of Iceland at the Ráðhúsið

MAP K2 ▪ Tjarnargata 11, Reykjavík ▪ 411 1111 ▪ Open 8am–7pm Mon–Fri, noon–6pm Sat & Sun

Plan or relive your travels with this enormous 3-D relief map of Iceland, complete with clearly marked glaciers, volcanoes and fjords. Finish with admiring the ducks and swans at Tjörnin lake (see p78).

9 Spectacular Waterfalls

Meltwater from Europe's largest glaciers feeds some mighty waterfalls where you can lose your-self in the noise and spray. The closest to Reykjavík are Gullfoss (see pp18–19) and Skógafoss (see p45), but it's worth the effort to reach Dynjandi (see p45) in the Westfjords and Dettifoss (see p44), Europe's largest waterfall, in the north.

10 Beaches

Iceland's beaches usually have black sand due to their proximity to volcanoes. The beaches are scenic yet isolated, especially the ones in Wesfjords. Popular white and yellow sand beaches can be found on the Snæfellsnes Peninsula and in and around Reykjavik. Go beachcombing (see p59) for hidden treasures.

TOP 10 BUDGET TIPS

Camping by Seljalandsfoss

1 Carry a weatherproof tent as the weather can change rapidly. Iceland's many campsites are usually well equipped and cost a fraction of a hotel bed. Camping Card (see p127) helps you save money at multiple campsites across the country.

2 A Hostelling International (YHA) card scores discounts at Iceland's many official youth hostels. Visit the website for details (www.hihostels.com).

3 Bring a sleeping bag with you to capitalize on some of the guest-houses' "sleeping bag" offer – accommodation provided at a significantly lower rate than that of a made-up bed.

4 If self-catering, bring your duty-free limit of alcohol and food.

5 Visit off-season (October–June). Some sights are closed or inaccessible, but accommodation and car-rental costs drop significantly.

6 Take advantage of online discounts from Icelandair, WOW Air or easyJet. Check websites for more information (www.icelandair.co.uk, www.wowair.co.uk, www.easyjet.co.uk).

7 Bus passes limit you to specific routes and timetables, but are cheaper than buying individual tickets.

8 Enjoy an inexpensive swim, sauna or hot tub session at public swimming pools around the country.

9 You can cycle around Iceland in a month, making savings on transport.

10 Buy locally produced smoked salmon, woollen jumpers or outdoor gear – still costly, but excellent value. Don't forget to claim tax refunds for items over ISK 6,000 (see p125).

🔟 Festivals

1 Myrkir Músíkdagar
Jan ■ www.darkmusicdays.is

Held at the end of January every year, the "Dark Music Days" festival brightens up Reykjavík's winter gloom with workshops and almost exclusively Icelandic contemporary music performances, ranging from avant- garde to opera.

2 Aldrei fór ég Suður
Apr ■ www.aldrei.is

This quirky music festival is held around Easter every year in Ísafjörður. Founded by a local musician Mugison and his father, it presents a wide range of Icelandic music, featuring popular acts ranging from the band Múm to local choirs.

3 Reykjavík Arts Festival
May ■ www.artfest.is

This biennial showcase of concerts, opera, dance and theatre has been held in mid-May since 1970. For three weeks every year the Reykjavík Arts Festival brings together major cultural venues and unconventional spaces throughout the city.

4 Songfest
Jul ■ MAP P6 ■ www.hafnar borg.is

This annual music festival offers concerts in Hafnarfjordur's Art Museum featuring classical music performed by top singers of Iceland.

5 Fiskidagurinn Mikli
Aug ■ MAP E2 ■ www. fiskidagurinnmikli.is

Early August (always the first or second Saturday of the month) sees Dalvík, a nondescript fishing village near Akureyri, draw the crowds with its "Great Fish Day", an eccentric social event. Apart from outdoor seafood buffets, look for homes displaying flaming torches – a sign that free fish soup is available.

6 Reykjavík Pride
Aug ■ www.reykjavikpride.is

Held annually since 1999, Reykjavík Pride goes from strength to strength, and is now one of the largest festivals in Iceland. For the last few years, up to one third of Iceland's population has attended the Saturday of Pride, when the parade winds through downtown Reykjavík.

7 Þjóðhátíð Vestmannaeyjar
Aug ■ www.dalurinn.is

Westman Islands Festival, held since 1874, is not for the faint-hearted. The festival includes camping for 4 days in August in a sodden volcano crater, being serenaded by a line-up of Icelandic rock at maximum decibels and skinny-dipping in the sea along with thousands of others.

Lively performance at the Aldrei fór ég Suður festival

Menningarnótt
Aug ■ www.menningarnott.is

One night in August is designated
Culture Night, during which downtown Reykjavík is closed to traffic
as stages are set up, performers
throng the streets and fireworks light
up the night sky. The entertainment is
mainly professional, with well-known
groups participating at times.

Menningarnótt fireworks

 **Djasshátíð – Reykjavík
Jazz Festival**
Sep ■ www.reykjavikjazz.is

The latest in jazz and blues come
to Reykjavík with a smattering of
international stars but the surprise
is the quality and abundance of local
talent. Do not miss the "Guitar Party"
event or the Jazz Parade which is
held on the opening day.

**Reykjavík International
Film Festival (RIFF)**
Sep ■ www.riff.is

A selection of the year's best
world cinema gets a screening at
the Reykjavík International Film
Festival. It is one of the biggest cultural events in Iceland and holds
events all around town. RIFF includes
programmes such as Icelandic
Panorama Section and side events
like Swim-in Cinema, Film Concert
and masterclasses with film-makers.

TOP 10 ICELANDIC MUSICIANS

Björk in concert

1 Björk
This singer is Iceland's best-known
musical export, though nowhere near
as popular at home as abroad.

2 Sigur Rós
The "post-rock" band Sigur Rós blends
elements of pop, classical and folk
music, and has unique vocals.

3 KK
Folk guitarist Kristján Kristjánsson is
the Arlo Guthrie of Iceland, quite often
teaming up with the veteran musician
Magnús Eiríksson.

4 Stefán Íslandi
Born in 1907, Stefán Íslandi performed
as an opera tenor in the US until his
death in 1994.

5 Sigrún Hjálmtýsdóttir
A leading opera soprano and jazz
singer, Sigrún Hjálmtýsdóttir has
performed with José Carreras and
Placido Domingo.

6 Kristinn Sigmundsson
Massive operatic bass, Sigmundsson
is one of Iceland's best known
international opera singers.

7 Mugison
A slide guitarist from the Westfjords,
Mugison, has an astounding voice
and performs Iceland's version of
fusion-delta blues.

8 Emiliana Torrini
Part Icelandic, part Italian,
sweet-voiced singer Torrini is the first
Icelander to top the German charts.

9 Bubbi Morthens
Bubbi Morthens is a mix of punk,
Bruce Springsteen and Johnny Cash.

10 Kristinn Árnason
A brilliant classical guitarist, Kristinn
Árnason also effortlessly manages
the crossover into rock music.

🔟 Offshore Islands

Imagine Peace Tower, Viðey

1 Viðey

Key historical figures have settled on this flat speck of land just off Reykjavík *(see p78)*, among them the country's last Catholic bishop, Jón Arason, and sheriff Skúli Magnússon, who built Iceland's first stone house here in 1755. Today it is a stage for the circular Imagine Peace Tower in memory of John Lennon.

2 Lundey

MAP P5 ■ Cruises from Reykjavík ■ www.elding.is

There are plenty of places called Lundey around Iceland – the name means "Puffin Island" – but this is the closest spot to Reykjavík where you can actually see the birds in question, at least while they are nesting between April and August. You cannot land here, but cruises circle Lundey daily in summer.

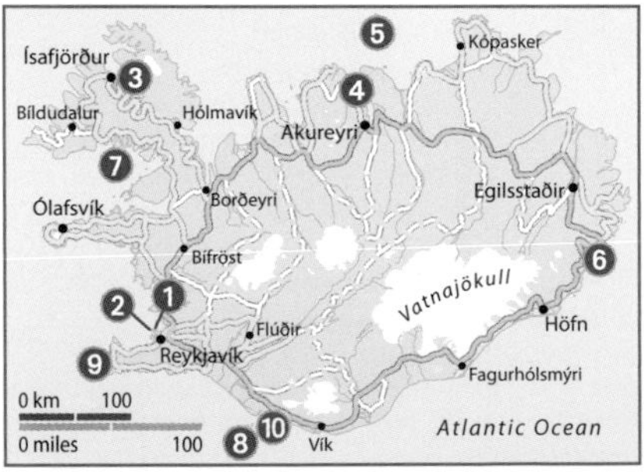

3 Vigur

MAP B2 ■ Daily ferry from Ísafjörður mid-Jun–late Aug ■ www.vesturferdir.is

Out in the Westfjords, this remote elongated islet makes a great half-day trip from Ísafjörður to see Arctic terns, puffins and especially eider ducks, whose warm, insulating down is commercially gathered for stuffing duvets and jackets. Only discarded chest feathers are collected and the birds are not harmed.

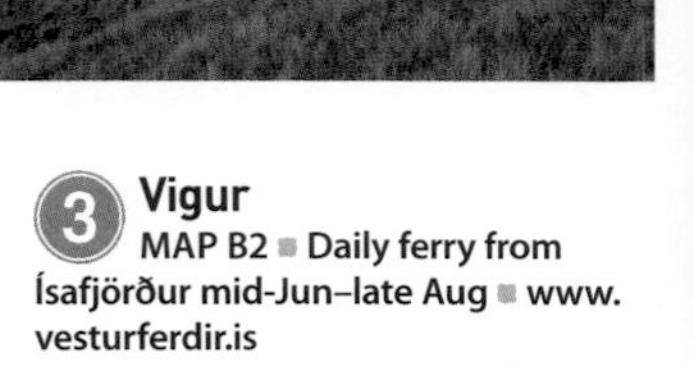

One of Vigur's eider ducks

4 Hrísey

MAP E2 ■ Daily ferry from Árskógssandur (up to 9 times a day) ■ www.hrisey.is/en

A peaceful and charming island in the Eyjafjörður – one of the longest fjords in Iceland – near the town of Akureyri. Hrísey is well known for its tractor sightseeing tours and rich bird life, including ptarmigans. The waters are also frequently visited by humpback whales.

A puffin on Grímsey

5 Grímsey

Iceland's northernmost point as well as the only part of the country that is actually crossed by the Arctic Circle – which means that the sun does not set here for a few days on either side of 21 June and does not rise at all in late December *(see p95)*. The island's cliffs are crowded with seabirds all year round which makes it a great day-trip destination.

6 Papey

Papey *(see p103)*, also known as "Monks' Island" is named after the Christian hermits who are believed to have been living here from when the Vikings arrived in the country. Today the 2 sq km (1 sq mile) island, rising just 60 m (197 ft) out of the sea, is home to thousands of puffins, a few sheep and the smallest church in the country.

7 Flatey

MAP E2 ■ Daily ferry from Stykkishólmur–Brjánslækur ■ www.seatours.is

Although hard to believe, this sleepy island, half-way across Breiðafjörður between Snæfellsnes and the Westfjords, housed an important 12th-century monastery. Later it became well-known for the *Flateyjarbók*, an illuminated medieval manuscript featuring the *Greenland Saga*, which was discovered on the island but is now kept in Reykjavík's Culture House. The east of the island is now a reserve for nesting seabirds.

8 Surtsey

MAP C6

Surtsey dramatically popped out of the waves during an underwater volcanic eruption to the southwest of Heimaey in 1963. Following erosion over the years, the island is now around 1.5 km (1 mile) across. Scientists are studying Surtsey to see how plants and animals colonize new lands. It is a special UNESCO reserve and strictly off-limits.

9 Eldey

MAP B5

About 15 km (9 miles) off Iceland's southwesternmost tip, Eldey's distinctive, rocky, sheer-sided cliffs rise 77 m (250 ft) straight out of the Atlantic. The top forms a level platform, home to Europe's largest gannet colony. Sadly, this is also where the last known pair of great auks were killed in 1844.

10 Heimaey

MAP C6 ■ Daily ferry to Herjólfur from Þorlákshöfn or Landeyjahöfn ■ www.eimskip.is

This 3-km- (2-mile-) long island off the south coast has enough birds, volcanoes, Viking history and walks to occupy you for a couple of sunny days. The town of the same name occupies the north end of the island and is famous for being nearly annihilated during a volcanic eruption in 1973.

Heimaey, a picturesque island town

Iceland
Area by Area

**Multicoloured volcanic landscape,
Landmannalaugar, South Iceland**

🔟 Reykjavík

Statue, National Museum

The Reykjavík area covers the city centre, plus a handful of satellite suburbs. The city's tiny core consists of a historic precinct of lanes near the old harbour, easily covered on foot in a day. While the municipal buildings are made of stone or concrete – practical protection against the fierce winter winds – most of the area is residential, comprising wooden houses, weatherproofed in brightly coloured corrugated iron. Here you will find most of Iceland's shops, cafés, restaurants and nightclubs, alongside museums and galleries. A distinctive land-mark is Öskjuhlíð hill, with panoramic views of more distant sights and suburbs.

REYKJAVÍK

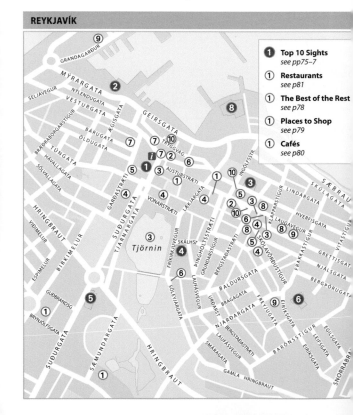

1 **Top 10 Sights**
see pp75–7

1 **Restaurants**
see p81

1 **The Best of the Rest**
see p78

1 **Places to Shop**
see p79

1 **Cafés**
see p80

1 Landnámssýningin (Settlement Exhibition)

MAP K2 ■ Aðalstræti 16 ■ 411 6370 ■ Open 9am–6pm daily ■ Adm ■ www.reykjavikcitymuseum.is

This impressive exhibition comprises the in-situ remains of a large Viking-age longhouse, possibly belonging to Iceland's first settler, Norwegian Ingólfur Arnarson (see p36), who sailed to Iceland around AD 870. There are virtually no other contemporary remains in such good condition. Its location under the capital's streets makes it even more incredible.

2 Historic Midtown and Harbour

MAP K1

Midtown is the site of Iceland's first Viking settlement and the

Historic buildings, midtown Reykjavík

city's oldest building (on Lækjatorg Square). A statue of Jón Sigurðsson (see p37) faces the 1881 Parliament House, which replaced the Alþing's home at Þingvellir. Visit the old harbour, Saga Museum as well as a whaling fleet.

3 Safnahúsið (Culture House)

MAP L2 ■ Hverfisgata 15 ■ 545 1400 ■ Open May–mid-Sep: 10am–5pm daily; mid-Sep–Apr: 10am–5pm Tue–Sun ■ On-site café ■ Guided tours available ■ www.nationalmuseum.is

As a part of the National Museum of Iceland, Safnahúsið gives an insight into the country's heritage through paintings, objects and archival materials, such as books and maps.

Medieval manuscript, Safnahúsið

4 Listasafn Íslands (National Gallery)

MAP L3 ■ Fríkirkjuvegur 7 ■ 515 9600 ■ Open summer: 10am–5pm daily; winter: 11am–5pm Tue–Sun ■ www.listasafn.is

The nation's main collection of art concentrates on early 20th-century Icelandic painters. Listasafn Íslands (see p40) continually rotates the estimated 10,000 works.

0 km   3
0 miles   3

Viðey ⑧

Reykjavík ●
Area of
main map

⑤
⑥ ⑩
④
⑩

5 km (3 miles) ⑦   ● Kópavogur

SÆBRAUT
②
BORGARTÚN
SKÚLAGATA   MIÐTÚN   HÁTÚN   NÓATÚN
HÖFÐATÚN
LAUGAVEGUR
LAUGAVEGUR
BRAUTARHOLT
SKIPHOLT
ÞVERHOLT
STÓRHOLT   NÓATÚN
②
350 metres
(383 yards)
HÁTEIGSVEGUR
FLÓKAGATA
⑦
0 metres   400
0 yards   400

5 Þjóðminjasafn Íslands (National Museum)

MAP K3 ■ Suðurgata 41 ■ 530 2200 ■ Open May–mid-Sep: 10am–5pm daily; mid-Sep–Apr: 11am–5pm Tue–Sun ■ Adm ■ www.national museum.is

Documenting Iceland's history and culture from the earliest evidence of settlement to the present, the museum *(see p40)* offers interactive learning opportunities for visitors. Whether it is Viking graves, medieval statues from churches or modern-day objects, there is something for everyone in this interesting exhibition covering the museum's two floors.

6 Hallgrímskirkja

MAP M3 ■ Hallgrímstorg 1 ■ 510 1000 ■ Open 9am–5pm daily ■ Cathedral free; tower adm ■ www.hallgrimskirkja.is

The largest in Iceland, this 74-m- (240-ft-) high church took 40 years to build and resembles a volcanic formation, covered in hexagonal pillars. The sound of the stunning church organ, fitted with 5,275 pipes, is a highlight. Take the lift to the tower for views over Reykjavík's colourful rooftops and Leifur Eiríksson's statue.

Leifur Eiríksson

THE SETTLEMENT OF REYKJAVÍK

When Ingólfur Arnarson first saw Iceland on his voyage from Norway in AD 870, he threw overboard his valuable wooden seat-posts and vowed to settle wherever they washed up. They were finally found in a broad, fertile, steamy inlet on the island's southwest, which Ingólfur named Reykjavík ("Smoky Bay").

---

7 Kjarvalsstaðir (Reykjavík Art Museum)

MAP N4 ■ Flókagata 24 ■ 411 6420 ■ Open 10am–5pm daily ■ Guided tours by arrangement ■ Adm ■ www.artmuseum.is

Jóhannes Kjarval (1885–1972), born in a tiny village in the north-east, studied painting in Europe. On returning to Iceland he began incorporating the landscapes into his brightly coloured paintings. Though considered Iceland's greatest artist, his work often controversially blended folklore, Christianity and paganism. Apart from his works, this museum also exhibits contemporary Icelandic and foreign art.

8 Harpa

MAP L2 ■ Austurbakki 2 ■ 528 5050 ■ Guided tours year-round ■ www.harpa.is

Harpa – Reykjavík's Concert Hall and Conference Centre – is the most important performance venue in the

Harpa, Reykjavík's Concert Hall and Conference Centre

country, and is home to the Iceland Symphony Orchestra, the Icelandic Opera and the Reykjavík Big Band. With a façade by artist Olafur Eliasson, it is a symbol of the revitalization of Reykjavík's historic waterfront and of Iceland's dynamism.

Perlan's mirrored-glass dome

9 Perlan
MAP M6 ▪ Öskjuhlíð ▪ Bus 18 from Hlemmur ▪ Exhibition: 8am–7pm daily; observation deck: 8am–8pm daily ▪ Adm ▪ www. perlanmuseum.is

Just south of the city centre, wooded Öskjuhlíð hill is covered in a network of walking and cycling tracks. The summit is capped by the mirrored-glass dome of Perlan ("the Pearl"). This imaginative building, made from converted cylindrical water tanks, has fabulous city panoramas from the outside observation deck. Inside, a permanent exhibition called Wonders of Iceland provides insights into the country's nature through interactive technology and design.

10 Laugardalur Park and Recreation Area
MAP R4 ▪ Laugardalur ▪ Bus 14 from Hlemmur ▪ Pool: 411 5100 ▪ Open Apr–Aug: 6:30am–10pm Mon–Fri, 8am–10pm Sat & Sun ▪ Park free; activities adm

East of the city centre, Laugardalur Park is a great spot to join local families relaxing. The Botanic Gardens have a zoo full of native species and a duck pond. You can skate in winter at the adjacent sports centre. The naturally heated 50-m-(164-ft-) long outdoor pool, with three smaller play pools and hot tubs, is open year-round.

MORNING

Kick off the day the way many Icelanders do – by having a swim at the central Sundhöllin indoor pool. After a coffee at **Kaffitár** on Bankastræti, head for the **Þjóðminjasafn Íslands** and get a solid grounding in Icelandic history, though don't burn out by trying to cover it all on a single trip. Amble down to get some fresh air and admire the birds at **Tjörnin** *(see p78)*, before ducking inside City Hall for a look at the giant relief map of the country, or to catch a lunchtime concert. Sit out on the grass at Austurvöllur Square to admire the humble Reykjavík Cathedral, the Art Deco Hótel Borg and the Parliament House. Then spend half an hour among Viking remains at the excellent **Landnámssýningin** *(see p75)*, which is located nearby.

AFTERNOON

Reboot your energy levels with a bowl of lamb soup at **Café Paris** *(see p80)*, then shop for jewellery, clothes or souvenirs along **Laugavegur** *(see p30)*. Head uphill, past a street of colourful houses on Klapparstígur, to take in the cityscape from the top of **Hallgrímskirkja**. If you have room for another museum, soak up some Saga-Age ambience at **Safnahúsið** *(see p75)*. Walk north to **Harpa** to take in a concert, or to see the striking Solar Voyager sculpture and historic **Höfði House** *(see p78)*. After dinner, visit some of the city's nightclubs – **Príkið** *(see p80)*, in the city centre, is the best place to start.

See map on pp74–5

The Best of the Rest

1 Norræna Húsið
MAP K4 ■ Sæmundargata 11
■ 551 7030 ■ Library open: 10am–
6pm Mon–Fri, 10am–5pm Sat & Sun;
exhibition room: times vary, check
website for details ■ www.nor
dichouse.is

Exhibitions, concerts and a library
devoted to Nordic culture.

Höfði House

2 Höfði House
MAP P2 ■ Borgartún

Mikhail Gorbachev and Ronald
Reagan ended the Cold War in
this house in 1986. Nearby
sculpture *Solar Voyager*
honours Viking travels.

3 Tjörnin
MAP K3

Locals bring their children
to spot the ducks, geese
and swans at this lake
in the city centre.

4 Alþingishúsið
MAP L2
■ Austurvöllur ■ 563 0500 ■ Check
for opening times ■ www.althingi.is

This building houses the national
parliament. Founded at Þingvellir
in AD 930, it relocated here in 1881.

5 Sigurjón Ólafsson Sculpture Museum
MAP Q1 ■ Laugarnestangi 70 ■ Buses
12 & 15 ■ 553 2906 ■ Open Jun–Aug:
2–5pm Tue–Sun; Sep–May: 2–5pm
Sat & Sun ■ www.lso.is

Once the studio of Sigurjón Ólafsson,
this building displays his sculptures
and hosts summer concerts.

6 Ásmundur Sveinsson Sculpture Museum
MAP Q4 ■ Sigtún ■ 411 6430
■ Open May–Sep: 10am–5pm daily;
Oct–Apr: 1–5pm daily ■ Adm
■ www.artmuseum.is

With its Mediterranean and African
influences, this building is as
interesting as the works of the
renowned sculptor displayed here.

7 Hafnarfjörður
MAP P6 ■ Bus 1 from
Hamraborg ■ www.hafnarfjordur.is,
www.fjorukrain.is

This seaside suburb of Reykjavík is
home to good restaurants and an
annual Viking festival.

8 Viðey
MAP P5 ■ mid-May–Sep: 8
ferries daily from Skarfabakka, and 2
daily from Reykjavík's Old Harbour
and Harpa ■ www.videy.com

Just off Reykjavík, this
grassy isle *(see p70)* boasts
Iceland's oldest stone
building (now a restaurant),
thousands of seabirds and
the Imagine Peace Tower.

Viðey seabird

9 The Einar Jónsson Sculpture Museum
MAP M3 ■ Eiríksgata ■ Open
10am–5pm Tue–Sun ■ Adm
■ www.lej.is

Three hundred plaster and
bronze statues by Iceland's first
modern sculptor, Einar Jónsson's
(1874–1954) are on display here.

10 Nauthólsvík Geothermal Beach
MAP M6 ■ Changing rooms open
mid-May–mid Aug: 11am–1pm
Mon–Fri (& 5–7pm Mon & Wed),
11am–3pm Sat

This yellow-sand beach is set right
on the waterfront south of the city
centre, complete with open-air hot
tubs and pool. No less fun for being
entirely artificial, its geothermal
pumps keep the water at 18ºC.

Places to Shop

1 Aurum
MAP L2 ■ Banakstræti 4
■ 551 2770 ■ www.aurum.is

Guðbjörg Kristín Ingvarsdóttir's jewellery is modelled on the landscape of Iceland, using precious metals to create delicate, fluid designs that are both modern and timeless.

2 The Viking
MAP L2 ■ Hafnarstræsti 1–3
■ 551 1250

Known for its friendly service and long opening hours, this gift shop has been in the same family for over 50 years. Now a chain with five stores across Iceland.

3 Thorvaldsens Bazar
MAP L2 ■ Austurstræti 4
■ 551 3509 ■ www.thorvaldsens.is

This charity shop has been in business for over a century and specializes in handmade Icelandic goods – knitted jumpers, local woodcarvings and silver jewellery.

4 Penninn Eymundsson
MAP L3 ■ Skólavörðustíg 11
■ 540 2350

This excellent bookshop offers a range of maps, from road atlases to hiking maps, as well as English-language books on Iceland and stationery. There is also a good café.

5 12 Tónar
MAP L3 ■ Skólavörðustíg 15
■ 511 5656

Selling music CDs and vinyl, this shop also hosts concerts (especially during the summer) by an eclectic inventory of local artists covering jazz, classical and pop.

6 Kraum
MAP L2 ■ Laugavegur 18b
■ 517 7797 ■ www.kraum.is

Local designers display and sell their clothes and accessories here. Look out for attractive silver and black lava jewellery.

Paper bowls at Kirsuberjatréð

7 Kirsuberjatréð
MAP L2 ■ Vesturgata 4
■ 562 8990 ■ www.kirs.is

This unique store, run by a women's cooperative, offers distinctly Icelandic garments, fish-skin accessories, glassware, jewellery and gifts.

8 Michelsen Watchmakers
MAP L2 ■ Laugavegur 15 ■ 511 1900 ■ www.michelsenwatch.com

Great old style watchmaker, with a workshop full of pre-digital timepieces in the process of being repaired. Sells Rolexes and other classic wristwatches.

9 Búrið – The Icelandic Pantry
MAP K1 ■ Grandagarður 35 ■ 551 8400 ■ blog.burid.is

Located in the old fishermen's huts by the harbour, this gourmet shop offers a tempting selection of cheeses and local specialities. It also holds workshops on Iceland's dairy history.

10 Kolaportið Flea Market
MAP L2 ■ Tryggvagata 19 ■ 562 5030 ■ Open 11am–5pm Sat & Sun

Join the locals in spending a couple of hours sifting through acres of household junk at this market and you might uncover unexpectedly stylish designer clothing. Good home-grown vegetables are for sale here, too.

See map on pp74–5 ←

Cafés

1 Café Paris
MAP L2 ■ Austurstræti 14
■ 551 1020 ■ Open 8:30am–10pm Sun–Thu, 8:30am–11pm Fri & Sat
Try the sandwiches at this popular café. Sit outside in good weather to enhance the Parisian ambience.

2 Prikið
MAP L2 ■ Bankastræti 12
■ 551 2866 ■ Open 8am–1am Mon–Thu, 11am–4:30am Fri & Sat, noon–1am Sun ■ www.prikid.is
This friendly café-diner (see pp66–7), frequented by an arty crowd, has a bar feel by night. There are hip-hop DJs at weekends.

3 Vegamót
MAP L3 ■ Vegamótstígur 4
■ 511 3040
Vegamót is busy at lunchtime and after dark. People-watch over a drink, or sample the Mediterranean menu.

4 Café Babalú
MAP L3 ■ 22, Skólavörðustígur
■ 555 8845
A quirky and colourful space, this café serves great coffee and cakes. It is frequented by a hip local crowd.

5 Grái Kötturinn
MAP L2 ■ Hverfisgata 16a
■ 551 1544 ■ Open 7:30am–2:30pm Mon–Fri, 8am–2:30pm Sat & Sun
Huge breakfasts are served at this trendy basement café. It's also a popular place to get coffee in the morning after a night out.

6 Hornið
MAP L2 ■ Hafnarstræti 15
■ 551 3340
In business since 1979, this family-run, cosy Italian pizzeria was one of the first places to serve espresso in Iceland. Their fresh seafood pastas are superb.

7 Café Stofan
MAP K2 ■ Aðalstræti
■ 567 1881
This warm spot operates as a café during the day and as a bar at night. Furnished with cosy couches and dining room tables, it offers barista-style coffee, Icelandic beers on tap as well as homemade vegetarian soups and bagels. They also have board games to play.

8 Boston
MAP M3 ■ Laugavegur 28b
■ 571 5781
With a welcoming, wooden interior and quirky decor, this bar is always well-populated. Enjoy your selection from the extensive drinks menu, whilst listening to jazz, golden oldies and new music releases.

9 Sandholt
MAP M3 ■ Laugavegur 36
■ 551 3524
Tasty sourdough breads, quiches, handmade chocolates, sandwiches and superb coffee are all served at this family-run bakery.

10 Mokka
MAP L3 ■ Skólavörðustíg 3a
■ 552 1174
Said to be the capital's oldest café (it opened in 1958), the no-frills Mokka is credited with spear-heading caffeine culture in Iceland.

Grái Kötturinn

Restaurants

PRICE CATEGORIES

For a three-course meal for one with half a bottle of wine (or equivalent meal), including taxes and extra charges.

Ⓚ under ISK5,000 ⓀⓀ ISK5,000–9,000
ⓀⓀⓀ over ISK9,000

① Grillið
MAP J3 ■ Radisson Blu Saga Hótel, Hagatorg, 107 Reykjavík ■ 525 9960 ■ www.grillid.is ■ Closed L ■ ⓀⓀ
Offering set menus, this restaurant (see p62) features dishes prepared by award-winning chefs.

② VOX
MAP R4 ■ Hilton Reykjavík Nordica, Suðurlandsbraut 2, 108 Reykjavík ■ 444 5050 ■ www.vox.is ■ ⓀⓀⓀ
This elegant fine dining restaurant (see p62) specializes in seafood. Try the Arctic char and trout roe.

③ Gló
MAP M3 ■ Laugavegur 20b ■ 553 111 ■ www.glo.is ■ ⓀⓀ
A pioneer of healthy, vegetarian and vegan cuisine, this unpretentious spot offers a daily-changing menu of four different main courses (one of which is usually raw), plus a tasty dessert.

④ Grillmarkaðurinn
MAP L2 ■ Lækjargata 2A, 101 Reykjavík ■ 571 7777 ■ Closed Sat & Sun L ■ www.grillmarkadurinn.is ■ ⓀⓀⓀ
The menu here (see p62) introduces dishes that are a smooth blend of the traditional and the modern.

⑤ Fiskmarkaðurinn
MAP K2 ■ Aðalstræti 12, 101 Reykjavík ■ 578 8877 ■ Closed L ■ ⓀⓀⓀ
Enjoy Japanese cuisine at this restaurant (see p63). The menu features a range of seafood dishes including sushi, maki and nigiri. Vegetarian options are available.

⑥ Holt Restaurant
MAP L3 ■ Hótel Holt, Bergstaðastræti 37, 101 Reykjavík ■ 552 5700 ■ Closed Sun–Tue ■ ⓀⓀ
Experienced chef Ragnar Eiríksson creates a fusion of traditional and modern cuisine (see p62). Book ahead.

⑦ Restaurant Reykjavík
MAP K2 ■ Vesturgata 2 ■ 552 3030 ■ ⓀⓀ
Known for its seafood, this beautiful old wooden warehouse overlooks Ingólfstorg square. Try the delicious seafood buffet.

Dishes at Restaurant Reykjavík

⑧ Sjávargrillið
MAP L3 ■ Skólavörðustíg 14, 101 Reykjavík ■ 571 1100 ■ Closed Mon–Sat D, Sun L ■ www.sjavar grillid.is ■ ⓀⓀ
Visit this classy candlelit restaurant to experience fine dining (see p63).

⑨ The Lobsterhouse
MAP L2 ■ Amtmannstíg 1 ■ 561 3303 ■ www.thelobsterhouse.is ■ ⓀⓀ
This intimate restaurant serves classic French cuisine with a refreshing Nordic twist.

⑩ Dill
MAP L2 ■ Hverfisgata 12 ■ 552 1522 ■ ⓀⓀⓀ
The first Icelandic restaurant to win a coveted Michelin star, Dill specializes in New Nordic Cuisine, pairing traditional dishes such as arctic char, lamb shanks and pork belly with barley, berries and kale.

See map on pp74–5 ←

🔟 West Iceland and the Snæfellsnes Peninsula

Heading north from Reykjavík, the highway follows the western coastline, famous for its stormy weather. Beyond Hvalfjörður and the exceptional Glymur falls are Akranes and Borgarnes, once home to the notorious Viking Egill Skallagrímsson. The 13th-century historian Snorri Sturluson lived (and was murdered) just inland at Reykholt, close to attractive waterfalls and more saga lore around Laxárdalur. Northwest of Borgarnes, the Snæfellsnes peninsula is dotted with fishing villages and its tip graced by Snæfellsjökull, the conical icecap covering a dormant volcano.

Búðir church

WEST ICELAND AND THE SNÆFELLSNES PENINSULA

Flatey ⑤
Breiðafjörður ⑤
Laugar
Laxárdalur ⑧
Hvammsfjörður
Búðardal
②
⑨ ⑩
Stykkishólmur ④
⑨
④
Hellissandur ① Rif
③ Ólafsvík Grundarfjörður ⑧ Kerlingarfjall 585 m
Snæfellsjökull National Park ⑦
⑥ Búðir
⑥
Hítará
Dritvík ⑧ Hellnar
Vegamót
Bifröst
⑤④
Reykholt
⑤
Borgarnes ①
① ② ③ ④
⑦
Faxaflói
Hvalfjörður ⑦ ⑩
⑦
Miðsandu
Akranes ⑨
Reykjavík
Mosfellsba

0 kilometres 30
0 miles 30

1 Borgarnes Settlement Center

MAP B4 ▪ Brákarbraut 13–15, Borgarnes ▪ 437 1600 ▪ Daily buses from Reykjavík to N1 in Borgarnes ▪ Open 10am–9pm daily ▪ Adm ▪ www.landnam.is

These exhibitions *(see p42)* explore the Saga of the Settlement Period (AD 870–930) of Iceland, which began with Viking settlers and ended when all free land was taken. A section celebrates Iceland's most famous viking and first poet Egill Skallagrímsson.

2 Hraunfossar, Barnafoss and Kaldidalur

MAP C4

About 15 km (9 miles) east up the valley from Reykholt on Route 518, the waterfalls at Hraunfossar and Barnafoss *(see p44)* – one gentle, the other violent – are worth a stop en route to Kaldidalur, a stark valley between the icy Ok and Þórisjökull peaks. The road is unsealed, but open in summer to ordinary vehicles (check conditions at *www.vegagerdin.is*).

Hraunfossar and Barnafoss waterfalls

3 Reykholt

MAP C4 ▪ Snorrastofa, Reykholt ▪ 433 8000 ▪ Open May–Aug: 10am–5pm daily; Sep–Apr: 10am–5pm Mon–Fri; also open by request ▪ Adm ▪ www.snorrastofa.is

The tiny hamlet of Reykholt belies its importance as the home of Snorri Sturluson (1179–1241), the historian who became tangled in Norway's bid to annex Iceland. Murdered by a rival with the support of the Norwegian king Hákon (he was trapped and killed in the cellar of his own house), his tale is told at the cultural and medieval centre Snorrastofa. His thermal bathing pool and the restored remains of the tunnel are located nearby.

4 Stykkishólmur

MAP B3 ▪ www.stykkisholmur. is ▪ Norska Húsið: 438 1640; open Jun–Aug: 11am–5pm daily; adm; www.norskahusid.is ▪ Library of Water: open Jun–Aug: 11am–5pm daily; Sep–May: 11am–5pm Tue–Sat; adm; www.vatnasafn.is

This town's wooden buildings recall its 19th-century port heyday, the best being Norska Húsið (Norwegian House). The nearby countryside is dotted with sites from *Eyrbyggja Saga (see p86)*. The Library of Water has 24 glass columns filled with water from Iceland's major glaciers.

Hvammstangi

Brú

Norðurá

Vatnsdalur

Arnarvatnsheiði

⑥
② Hraunfossar and Barnafoss
⑤ Húsafell

Langjökull

Ok △
0 m
② Kaldidalur

Skorradalsvatn

Skorradalsvatn

...garvatn

...gvallavatn

Snæfellsjökull, the icecapped volcano at the centre of the national park

5 Breiðafjörður and Flatey
MAP B3 ■ Sea Tours: www.sea
tours.is ■ Flatey: www.hotelflatey.is
Breiðafjörður – the huge, wide
bay separating the Snæfellsnes
peninsula from the Westfjords to
the north – is thick with islands
and rocky reefs, providing an ideal
breeding ground for marine birds.
From Stykkishólmur, you can
explore the bay on a tour with Sea
Tours (see p71), or go to Brjánslækur
in the Westfjords via Breiðafjörður's
largest island, Flatey, once home to
an important monastery. For a taste
of island life and bird-watching,
stay in Flatey's tiny village.

6 Búðir
MAP A4
Búðir is a minute place on the south
coast of Snæfellsnes, with just a
church and a hotel. One can enjoy
beautiful seascapes and views of
Snæfellsjökull (see pp26–7) from
here. The dark wooden church dates
from 1703. Its graveyard and boundaries are encroached upon by the
Búðahraun lava field, which is said to
be inhabited by creatures from local
folklore. Despite its remote location,
the romantic Hótel Búðir (see p130) is
famous for being a favourite of
Nobel Prize-winning author Halldór
Laxness. Don't miss the amazing
black-sand beach.

7 Snæfellsjökull National Park
Based around an icecapped
volcano, this national park (see
pp26–7) extends over rough, vegetated lava fields to a coastline
rich in birdlife. Hiking, skiing and
exploring local villages or Vatnshellir
lava cave (www.vatnshellir.is) are
all possible, and you can easily
circuit the park by car in a day.

8 Laxárdalur
MAP C3
This pretty valley along Route 59
is the setting for Laxdæla Saga, the
great tragic love story of Icelandic
literature. It tells of the beautiful
Guðrún Ósvífursdóttir and her four
husbands: the first she divorces,
but the rest perish due to witchcraft,
feuding and drowning, respectively,
while she becomes a nun. Only

EGIL'S SAGA

An interesting mixture of history,
folklore and political allegory, Egil's
Saga recounts the roller-coaster life of
Egill Skallagrímsson (AD 910–990), a
bully of a Viking who spent his youth
fighting the Norwegians and his old
age fighting everyone else, but was
nonetheless a magnificent poet. A
must-read, along with Njál's Saga and
Laxdæla Saga.

place names from that time survive, namely the church at Hjarðarholt, and the farmsteads at Goddastaðir and Höskuldsstaðir.

9 Akranes
MAP B5

Akranes, Iceland's oldest fishing port, is a good place to experience a down-to-earth, gritty Icelandic town. Fishing is still the main industry and the harbour and processing factory survive alongside the less romantic National Cement Works. The town is famous for its sports club, Íþróttabandalag Akranes, whose football team has won the Icelandic Championship 18 times. The engaging Akranes Folk Museum (see p86) and a charming lighthouse provide good reasons to visit, though their location is a 10-km (6-mile) detour off the highway.

10 Hvalfjörður
MAP C4

Most people use the tunnel under the bay to bypass the 30-km- (19-mile-) deep Hvalfjörður and miss some classic scenery, including Glymur (see p44), Iceland's highest waterfall. Hvalfjörður means "whale fjord", after the number of whales once seen here. It was a US naval base during World War II and the red barracks are now holiday homes.

Glymur waterfall

A DAY IN THE WEST

> ## MORNING

Drive north from Reykjavík around Kjalarnes, where the road is pinched between the sea and the Esja plateau. Avoid the 6-km- (4-mile-) long cross-fjord tunnel and follow Route 47 around **Hvalfjörður**. At the head of the fjord, take the 4-km (3-mile) gravel road inland, and then hike 5.5-km (3.5-mile), to where the Glymur waterfall cascades down the 200-m- (656-ft-) high cliffs. Continue around Hvalfjörður to rejoin Route 1 and continue to **Borgarnes** (see p83). Spend an hour at the Settlement Center, delving into the lives of Iceland's Viking pioneers. Don't miss out on the spooky dioramas downstairs, retelling the tale of Egil's Saga. Have a quick lunch at the good-value café here.

AFTERNOON

Make **Deildartunguhver** (see p48), Europe's largest thermal spring, the first stop of the afternoon, followed by a further historical halt at **Reykholt** (see p83), taking in the Heimskringla Museum, the church and old geothermal bathing pool. From here, follow Route 518 to **Hraunfossar** and **Barnafoss** (see p44), the latter is the setting for a tragic tale of two children who drowned in the rapids here while trying to cross over a lava bridge. Both falls are small but attractive. At this point you can retrace your route or (though this is an adventurous, summer-only option) follow gravel tracks south via **Kaldidalur** (see p83) to Þingvellir (see pp12–13) and then back to Reykjavík.

See map on pp82–3 ←

The Best of the Rest

1 Borg á Mýrum
MAP B4

Site of Egill Skallagrímsson's home, but nothing contemporary is left. The statue *Sonatorrek (Lament for my Dead Son)* is named after his poem.

Sonatorrek

2 Eiríksstaðir
MAP C3 ■
Eiríksstaðir, Haukadal, 371 Búðardalur ■ 434 1118 ■ Open Jun–Aug: 9am–6pm daily ■ Adm ■ www.eiriksstadir.is

The reconstructed longhouse of Viking Eiríkr Þorvaldsson, known as Eirik the Red, and his son Leifur, who explored Greenland and North America.

3 Pakkhúsið
MAP A3 ■ Ólafsbraut, Ólafsvík ■ 433 6930 ■ Open summer: noon–5pm daily; winter: by request ■ Adm

This 1844 warehouse contains a café and a folk museum. Photographs and fishing memorabilia outline the town's history.

4 Berserkjahraun
MAP B3

Eyrbyggja Saga tells how a warrior was promised a local man's daughter if he cleared a path through this lava field, but was murdered once he completed the task.

5 Húsafell
MAP C4

Picturesque spread of woodland and meadows east of Reykholt, with an old church, open-air geothermal swimming pool and petrol station serving the scattered community of summer houses used by holiday-makers. Home to artist Páll Guðmundsson.

6 Surtshellir
MAP C4

Large subterranean cave near Húsafell, named after the giant Surtur. Later used by outlaws, who hid stolen livestock here.

7 Akranes Folk Museum
MAP B5 ■ Garðaholt 3, Akranes ■ 433 1150 ■ Open mid-May–mid-Sep: 10am–5pm daily; mid-Sep–mid-May by group reservation ■ Adm ■ www.museum.is

This museum showcases folk artifacts and sports exhibits.

8 Kerlingarfjall
MAP B3

Route 56 to Stykkishólmur crosses Kerlingarfjall, a mountain said to be haunted by the ghost of a female troll, who turned to stone on her way back from a fishing expedition.

9 Stykkishólmur Church
MAP B3 ■ Open 10am–5pm daily ■ Adm for recitals

Shaped like an abstract ship, the church holds music recitals from June to August.

10 Glanni
MAP C4

A pretty cascade over black lava on the Norðurá salmon river near Bifröst. You can see salmon swim upstream.

Berserkjahraun lava field

Places to Eat

PRICE CATEGORIES
For a three-course meal for one with half
a bottle of wine (or equivalent meal),
including taxes and extra charges.

Ⓚ under ISK5,000 ⓀⓀ ISK5,000–9,000
ⓀⓀⓀ over ISK9,000

Hótel Búðir

1 Viðvík
MAP A3 ▪ Hellissandur 360
▪ 436 1026 ▪ ⓀⓀ

Set against the spectacular views of
the Snæfellsjökull glacier and the
ocean, Viðvík has a top-notch menu
that is updated seasonally. Try the
langoustine bisque and cod dishes.

2 Hótel Hamar
MAP B4 ▪ Ⓚ

Not the most formal of fine dining
restaurants, Hótel Hamar (see p130)
offers a gourmet menu that includes
the catch-of-the-day with chickpeas,
and tomatoes. The restaurant has
beautiful views of Borgarfjörður fjord.

3 Settlement Center
MAP B4 ▪ Brákarbraut 13–15,
Borgarnes ▪ 437 1600 ▪ Ⓚ

Great for an inexpensive meal – you
can choose from the extensive à
la carte menu or the lunch buffet,
which has a variety of salads, pasta
and freshly baked bread.

4 N1
MAP B4 ▪ Brúartorg,
Borgarnes ▪ Ⓚ

An alternative to the ever-crowded
N1 petrol station canteen – known by
the same name – N1 is a good place
to grab a quick sandwich or a pizza
during the day.

5 Fosshótel Reykholt
MAP C4 ▪ 320 Reykholt ▪ 435
1260 ▪ www.fosshotel.is ▪ Ⓚ

A top choice in Reykholt – the
restaurant offers simple soups,
grills and pan-fried Arctic char
with sweet potato puree and
black lentils. Guests at the hotel
also get to use the spa.

6 Hótel Búðir
MAP A4 ▪ ⓀⓀ

The restaurant in Hotel Búðir (see
p130), serves fresh lamb and seafood
dishes in a smart setting. It is cheaper
than similar Reykjavík venues.

7 Hótel Glymur
MAP C3 ▪ Hvalfjörður ▪ 430
3100 ▪ www.hotelglymur.is ▪ Ⓚ

Smart retreat with an accomplished
menu – carpaccio beef, pan-seared
trout and home-made ice cream.
The café serves tasty snacks.

8 Fjöruhúsið
MAP A4 ▪ Hellnar, Snæfellsnes
▪ 435 6844 ▪ Closed Dec–May ▪ Ⓚ

A small café with good-value meals.
It is famous for fish soup, coffee,
cakes and harbour views.

9 Bjargarsteinn
MAP B3 ▪ Sólvellir 15,
Grundarfjörður ▪ 438 6770 ▪ Closed
L ▪ www.bjargarsteinn.is ▪ Ⓚ

This is a cosy family-owned
restaurant overlooking the Kirkjufell
mountain. They offer both traditional
and contemporary dishes such as
the fish of the day which is popular.
Local and seasonal ingredients are
used whenever possible.

10 Narfeyrarstofa
MAP B3 ▪ Aðalgata 3,
Stykkishólmur ▪ 438 1119 ▪ www.
narfeyrarstofa.is ▪ Ⓚ

Narfeyrarstofa is set in an old wooden
building with a tiny lounge. Try the
scallops from Breiðarfjörður Bay, pan-
fried in butter, garlic and chili, served
with Icelandic barley.

See map on pp82–3 ←

🔟 The Westfjords

There is grandeur in the high, flat-topped mountains, brilliant blue seas and rugged coastline of the Westfjords, located in the extreme northwest of Iceland. For the region's scattered communities, life has been tough given the minimal infrastructure outside Ísafjörður, the only sizable town. The attractions of the area are mostly strung along the west coast between the Látrabjarg bird cliffs and Ísafjörður. Though the eastern Strandir coast offers a low-key beauty, inland views are filled by snow-streaked plateaus. Visit in summer when the buses run from Reykjavík and the roads are open: you can fly into Ísafjörður but from there you will need to drive onward.

Thermal pool, Flókalundur

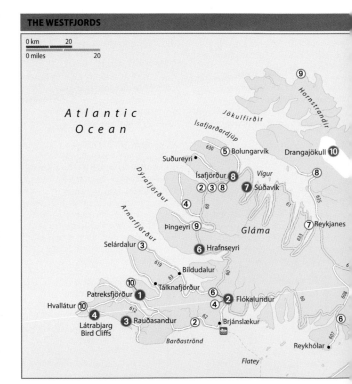

THE WESTFJORDS

Atlantic Ocean

Jökulfirðir

Ísafjarðardjúp

Dýrafjörður

Arnarfjörður

Hornstrandir

630 ⑤ Bolungarvík — Drangajökull 🔟

Suðureyri •

Ísafjörður ⑧ — Vígur — ⑧
②③⑧ — ⑦ Súðavík

④

Þingeyri ⑨ — *Gláma* — ⑦ Reykjanes

Selárdalur ③ — ⑥ Hrafnseyri

Bíldudalur

🔟
Patreksfjörður ① Tálknafjörður ⑥ ② Flókalundur
④
Hvallátur 🔟
④ ③ Rauðasandur ② • Brjánslækur
Látrabjarg
Bird Cliffs
Barðaströnd ⑥

Reykhólar •

Flatey

Wild flowers near Patreksfjörður

1 Patreksfjörður
MAP A2

Named after St Patrick, this sizable fishing village on Route 62 is where Iceland's trawling industry started in the early 20th century. It is famous for attacks by Basque whalers during the early 17th century. It is also the last place to stock up with provisions and fuel if you are heading to the Látrabjarg bird cliffs or the beach at Breiðavík (see pp28–9), which is southwest on Route 612.

1	**Top 10 Sights** see pp89–91
1	**Places to Eat** see p93
1	**The Best of the Rest** see p92

Norðurfjörður
• Gjögur
Djúpavík
643
Húnaflói
Skagaströnd •
Hólmavík
Hrútafjörður
Þingeyrar •
Hvammstangi

2 Flókalundur
MAP B2 ■ Vatnsfjörður Nature Reserve: www.ust.is

Flókalundur ("Flóki's Wood") is a tiny south-coast area on Route 62, named after the Viking Flóki Vilgerðarson. He endured a harsh winter here around AD 860 and, on climbing nearby Lómfell, he saw the fjord below choked with ice and gave "Ice Land" its name. The surrounding wetlands, dwarf forest and barren basalt highlands are now protected as the Vatnsfjörður Nature Reserve. You can explore it using Hótel Flókalundur (see p93) as a summertime base.

3 Rauðasandur
MAP A3

Seals are frequently seen at this cinnamon-coloured beach on the southwesternmost peninsula of the Westfjords, along the unsealed Route 614. Arctic skuas nest on the grasslands behind the spit. As well as offering wildlife, the ruins of Sjöundá farm lie 5 km (3 miles) east of the beach. Gunnar Gunnarsson's novel Svartfugl (Blackbird) is based on a double murder there in 1802.

4 Látrabjarg Bird Cliffs

This is among the most stirring sights in Iceland (see pp28–9). Millions of seabirds cram into the cliffs in summer – the noise and stench are remarkable. The dramatic landscape, empty beaches and isolated buildings evoke the hardships of rural life. Local buses travel here in summer.

The dramatic Látrabjarg bird cliffs

⑤ Hólmavík Museum of Sorcery and Witchcraft

MAP C2 ▪ Höfðagata 8, 510 Hólmavík ▪ 897 6525, 451 3525 ▪ Open 9am–6pm daily ▪ Adm ▪ www.galdrasyning.is

Situated on the southeast coast, Hólmavík has a Museum of Sorcery and Witchcraft that draws on the district's reputation for the dark arts – during the 17th century 20 people (only one was female) were burned at the stake. The museum has models, trinkets, an audio tour and a demonstration of spell-casting. It runs a "Sorcerer's Cottage" 28 km (17 miles) up the coast, which shows how people lived in the 17th century. Grab a bite at the on-site restaurant, Galdur.

⑥ Hrafnseyri

MAP B2 ▪ 456 8260 ▪ Open Jun–Sep: 11am–6pm daily ▪ Adm ▪ www.hrafnseyri.is

Hrafnseyri is a church and turf farmhouse overlooking the sea at Arnarfjörður. It is the birthplace of Jón Sigurðsson (1811–79), whose campaign for Iceland's independence from Denmark restored the parliament and enacted a self-governing constitution. His birthday, 17 June, is celebrated as National Day. In the main building of the farmhouse is an exhibition dedicated to Sigurðsson's life. The turf house is a replica of his home, and coffee and cakes are served here. Don't miss the Dynjandi waterfall, 15 km (9 miles) to the south.

TIMBER FROM THE SEA

Iceland has always been short of home-grown timber for building boats and houses, which from Viking times has placed great demand on driftwood. Fortunately, plenty washes up around the country, particularly along the Westfjords' pebbly Strandir coast, whose beaches are often strewn with tree trunks that have floated all the way from Siberia.

⑦ Súðavík Arctic Fox Centre

MAP B2 ▪ Eyrardal, Súðavík ▪ 456 4922 ▪ Open May–Sep: 9am–6pm daily; Oct–Apr: 10am–2pm Mon–Fri ▪ Adm ▪ www.arcticfoxcenter.com

Originally the only mammal to inhabit Iceland was the Arctic fox, which probably drifted here from Greenland on ice floes. Smaller than the European red fox, the Arctic fox can either have a brown coat all year, or a grey one in summers and white in winters. The Arctic Fox Centre, located at Eyrardalur farm, 20 km (12 miles) around the coast from Ísafjörður, explores the animal's biology and relationship with man. Rescued foxes can be found in the centre's garden.

Dynjandi waterfall, south of Hrafnseyri

8 Ísafjörður

MAP B2 ■ Tourist office: 450 8060; www.isafjordur.is ■ Westfjords Maritime Museum: Turnhús, Suðurgata, Ísafjörður; 848 5030; open mid-May–mid-Sep: 9am–5pm daily; adm; www.nedsti.is

The region's main town, Ísafjörður is a mass of narrow streets and old buildings. Chief among these is the Turnhús, which houses the Westfjords Maritime Museum (see p43). Across the Ísafjarðardjúp straits, the uninhabited Hornstrandir peninsula offers the ultimate hiking challenge. Boats run out here and to little Vigur island (see p70) through the summer.

Traditional buildings, Ísafjörður

9 Norðurfjörður
MAP C2

At the end of Route 643 up the east Strandir coast, Norðurfjörður is small, even for the Westfjords, but the scenery is stunning and makes the drive along gravel roads worthwhile. The town is backed by the 646-m- (2,125-ft-) high Krossnesfjall hill and looks out to the sea across Norðurfjörður bay. About 4 km (2 miles) away lies Krossneslaug, a beachside swimming pool fed by a hot spring.

10 Drangajökull
MAP B2

The area's sole permanent icecap, Drangajökull makes a splendid sight on the top of a high plateau. During the 18th century it covered local farms but has now shrunk. The best view is along the dead-end Route 635 to Kaldalónsjökull, a glacier descending off larger Drangajökull. It is an hour's walk from Kaldalón (see p92).

A DAY IN THE WESTFJORDS

▶ MORNING

Arriving at Brjánslækur by ferry from Stykkishólmur on the Snæfellsnes peninsula (see p83), drive north up Route 62 to Flókalundur (see p89). Fuel up and buy something for a picnic lunch here before turning onto Route 60. This good gravel road climbs up to the Dynjandisheiði plateau and then drops abruptly to the coast at the stunning and noisy Dynjandi waterfall (see p45), a great place to stretch your legs and spend an hour exploring the multilevel cascades (the lighting is best here in the evening). A grassy area at the foot of the falls makes a perfect spot for a picnic.

AFTERNOON

Leaving Dynjandi waterfall, carry on around the bay to Hrafnseyri, birthplace of Jón Sigurðsson (see p37), and drop in at the museum celebrating the life of this great Icelandic patriot. From here it is a further 65 km (40 miles) to Ísafjörður via Þingeyri (the Westfjords' oldest trading town), two mountain passes and a lengthy single-lane tunnel – there are passing bays inside, but traffic is never heavy. Once at Ísafjörður, track down your accommodation and then visit the Westfjords Maritime Museum (see p43) inside the old Turnhús or simply stroll down to the harbour, where you can usually spot marine ducks. The nearby Hotel Ísafjörður (see p93) is an ideal place for a hearty evening meal.

See map on pp88–9 ←

The Best of the Rest

Djúpavík's coastline

1 Djúpavík
MAP C2

Wild, beautiful Djúpavík, halfway along Strandir's coast, is dominated by a century-old shipwreck and a former herring processing factory that hosts exhibitions in the summer.

2 Reiðskörð
MAP A3

Route 62 runs past this tall and fragmented volcanic dyke at Barðaströnd, the bay south of the Westfjords.

3 Selárdalur
MAP A2 ▪ Arnarfjörður

Self-taught artist Samúel Jónsson (1884–1969) lived in this isolated valley at the end of Route 619, and left behind a bizarre range of sculptures and buildings.

4 Skrúður
MAP A2 ▪ Núpur

Set at the foot of a valley on Route 624, Iceland's oldest botanic garden was founded as a teaching garden in 1909 by Reverend Sigtryggur Guðlaugsson.

5 Bolungarvík
MAP B1 ▪ Ósvör Maritime Museum: 892 5744, 456 7005; open by appointment; www.osvor.is ▪ Natural History Museum: open by appointment; 456 7005, 860 374; www.nab.is

This fishing port has the 19th-century rowing boat at the Ósvör Maritime Museum. The Natural History Museum features stuffed mammals and birds, stones and other collections.

6 Pennugil
MAP B2

This narrow canyon on the Penná river is about a 30-minute walk from Flókalundur on a marked trail. There is a hot spring feeding the river which is suitable for bathing.

7 Reykjanes
MAP B2

The hamlet of Reykjanes has a geothermal pool and sauna.

8 Kaldalón
MAP B2

Kaldalón ("Cold Lagoon") is fed by Drangajökull glacier (see p91). It inspired local musician Sigvaldi Stefánsson (1881–1946) to call himself Kaldalóns.

9 Hælavíkurbjarg
MAP B1

This vertical 258-m- (847-ft-) high cliff between Hælavík and Hornvík islets is only accessible by boat. It is one of the area's major bird colonies, along with Látrabjarg and Hornbjarg.

10 Hvallátur
MAP A2 ▪ www.breidavik.is

Iceland's westernmost settlement (see p29) comprises a farm and hotel at Breiðavík beach. It played a central role in the *Dhoon* shipwreck rescue in 1947.

Places to Eat

PRICE CATEGORIES

For a three-course meal for one with half a bottle of wine (or equivalent meal), including taxes and extra charges.

Ⓚ under ISK5,000 ⓀⓀ ISK5,000–9,000
ⓀⓀⓀ over ISK9,000

1 Hótel Djúpavík

MAP C2 ■ Djúpavík, Strandir ■ 451 4037 ■ www.djupavik.com ■ ⓀⓀ

Friendly with a fantastic location, this hotel serves tasty, home-cooked food in a cosy, wood-beamed dining room. Try the pan-fried cod served with rice and salad.

2 Tjöruhúsið

MAP B2 ■ Neðstakaupstað 400, Ísafjörður ■ 456 4419 ■ Ⓚ Ⓚ

This family-owned spot serves the catch-of-the-day – usually wolf-fish, cod or halibut – as well as a langoustine and tomato-based fish soup, and a traditional Icelandic fish stew. Children under the age of 14 eat for free.

3 Hamraborg Snack Bar

MAP B2 ■ Hafnarstræti 7, Ísafjörður ■ 456 3166 ■ Ⓚ

This fast-food place serves burgers, sandwiches, pizza and *pylsur* (hot dogs) with a variety of toppings including remoulade, onions and tomato sauce.

4 Hótel Flókalundur

MAP A2 ■ Vatnsfirði 451, Patreksfjörður ■ 456 2011 ■ Closed Sep–May ■ www.flokalundur.is ■ Ⓚ–ⓀⓀ

This small hotel-restaurant offers lunch specials, smaller meals as well as a dinner menu.

5 Hótel Laugarhóll

MAP B3 ■ Strandir, Bjarnarfjörður ■ 451 3380 ■ www.laugarholl.is ■ ⓀⓀ

Pleasant hotel in a marvellous setting with a thermal pool and hiking trails within walking distance. Its excellent restaurant has set menus.

6 Hótel Bjarkalundur

MAP B3 ■ Reykhólahreppi ■ 894 1295 ■ ⓀⓀ

This welcoming restaurant serves traditional Icelandic dishes made from fresh local ingredients.

7 Café Riis

MAP C2 ■ Hafnarbraut 39, Hólmavík ■ 451 3567 ■ Closed Sep–May ■ Ⓚ

The best restaurant on the Strandir coast, serving pan-fried chicken breast, roast trout and lamb fillets. Also offers pizzas, burgers and cakes.

8 Hótel Ísafjörður

MAP B2 ■ 456 3360 ■ ⓀⓀ

The hotel-restaurant *(see p130)*, Við Pollinn, has Nordic decor and offers tasty local fare such as catch of the day, grilled lamb and seafood soup.

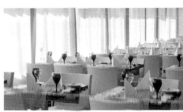

Hótel Ísafjörður

9 Simbahöllin

MAP B2 ■ Fjarðargata 5, 470 Þingeyri ■ 899 6659 ■ Closed Oct–mid-May ■ www.simbahollin.is ■ Ⓚ

Charming café set inside an old wooden grocery store, with excellent coffee, soups, stews and a local take on Belgian waffles. The owners offer horse-riding tours and rent out bikes.

10 Tjöruhúsið

MAP B2 ■ Neðstakaupstað, 400 Ísafjörður ■ 456 4419 ■ ⓀⓀ

Set on Ísafjörður's waterfront, Tjöruhúsið *(see pp62–3)* is an excellent seafood restaurant. They don't go by a specific menu and usually serve the catch-of-the-day. Children under 14 can dine here for free.

See map on pp88–9 ←

TOP 10 North Iceland

Rich in history and wildlife and with an amazing landscape, North Iceland could easily make for a week-long trip all of its own. There is the pleasant regional capital city, Akureyri, with its fjord setting and old buildings. An abundance of wildfowl and volcanic attractions around Lake Mývatn combined with the picturesque Húsavík's laid-back charm, unusual museums and whale-watching cruises make it worth a visit. Jökulsárgljúfur's incredible gorge system and waterfalls, not to mention a wealth of antique farms, churches as well as saga sites, some of them – such as Hólar – are central to Icelandic history and culture. Almost all the sights in this region are located on, or easy to reach from, Route 1, making it very accessible.

Beautiful Rauðhólar

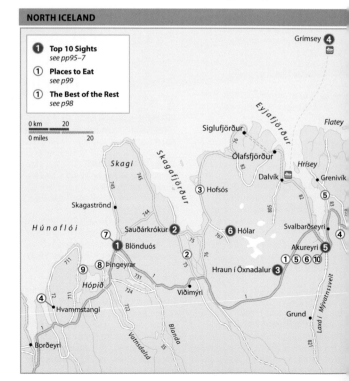

NORTH ICELAND

1. **Top 10 Sights**
   see pp95–7

1. **Places to Eat**
   see p99

1. **The Best of the Rest**
   see p98

0 km 20
0 miles 20

Grímsey ④

Eyjafjörður

Flatey

Siglufjörður

Ólafsfjörður

Skagi

Skagafjörður

Hrísey

Dalvík

Grenivík ⑤

③ Hofsós

805

Skagaströnd

744

Svalbarðseyri

Sauðárkrókur ②

⑥ Hólar

④

Húnaflói

⑦

745

② ①⑤⑥⑩ Akureyri ⑤

① Blönduós

②

⑨ ⑧ Þingeyrar

731

Hraun í Öxnadalur ③

Hópið

Viðimýri

Laxdárdalur Mývatnssveit

④

Hvammstangi

Grund

Vatnsdalsá

Blanda

821

Borðeyri

Atmospheric old buildings, Sauðárkrókur town square

1 Blönduós
MAP D2

This port has a striking church, with steeply sloping concrete walls echoing the shape of the mountains. Other attractions include trips to see seals and birdlife in the bay and, 15 km (9 miles) west at Vatnsdalshólar, an expanse of mounds formed during an earthquake, is the site of Iceland's last execution in 1830.

2 Sauðárkrókur
MAP D2 ■ Drangey boat trips with Viggó Jónsson; 821 0090; May–Aug; www.drangey.net

The appeal of Sauðárkrókur comes from the tiny knot of atmospheric old buildings that surround the town square, principally the church and Hótel Tindastóll (www.hoteltindastoll. com), which are said to be haunted. The coast here features in *Grettir's Saga*: Grettislaug, a lovely seaside thermal bathing pool, is where he recovered after swimming over from Drangey island in search of fresh embers to reignite his own fire.

3 Hraun í Öxnadalur
MAP E2

This farm in the deep Ox Valley is famous as the birth-place of poet and biologist Jónas Hallgrímsson (1807–45). His romantic verses extolling the landscape influenced the way Icelanders, most of whom then lived in poverty in rural turf buildings, began to perceive their country as glorious, rather than embarrassing.

4 Grímsey
MAP E1 ■ Daily flights from Akureyri Jun–late Aug: Mon, Tue & Fri–Sun; rest of the year: Tue, Fri & Sun only; boats from Dalvík Sep–May: four times a week; Jun–Aug: five times a week ■ www.grimsey.is/en

The only part of Iceland inside the Arctic Circle (see p71), Grímsey is 40 km (25 miles) north of the mainland, and is little more than 3 km (2 miles) long, with tiny Sandvík in the south being the only settlement. In the north, its sheer cliffs are packed with nesting seabirds in summer.

5 Akureyri
MAP E2 ■ Tourist info: www.visitakureyri.is ■ Strandgata 12; 450 1050

Iceland's largest settlement after Reykjavík, with a population of over 18,500, Akureyri is a relaxed town with a pretty harbour, shops, cafés and restaurants. Looming over everything is Akureyrarkirkja, a picturesque church, with stunning stained-glass windows (some brought from England's old Coventry Cathedral) and modern depictions of famous Icelanders. Don't miss the Botanic Gardens, where both native and imported plants thrive, Akureyri Swimming Pool, with its geothermal heated water and hot tubs, or the Akureyri Art Museum in the Old Town.

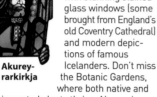

Akureyrarkirkja

6 Hólar
MAP D2 ■ Tourist office: 455 6333; open Jun–Aug 10am–10pm daily ■ www.holar.is

More fully known as Hólar í Hjaltadal, this was once the largest settlement in northern Iceland thanks to the monastery and religious school founded in 1106 by bishop Jón Ögmundsson, which attracted scholars and monks

GRETTIR'S SAGA

Grettir's Saga recounts the life of Grettir Ásmundarson, a fierce warrior who performs great deeds in the service of others, but is haunted by a *draugur*, or evil ghost. Grettir ends his life as an outlaw on Drangey island, where he is finally killed by his enemies.

from across Europe. These institutions survived the Reformation – which saw the execution of Hólar's last Catholic bishop, Jón Arason – and today the cathedral *(see p39)* and the college specializing in aquaculture, rural tourism and horse science are the sole buildings here.

7 Húsavík
MAP E2 ■ Whale-watching tours: www.gentlegiants.is and www.northsailing.is ■ Whale Museum: Hafnarstétt 1, Húsavík; 414 2800; open Jun–Aug 8:30am–6:30pm daily; May & Sep 9am–6pm daily; Oct & Apr 10am–4pm daily; Nov–Mar 10am–4pm Mon–Fri; adm; www.whalemuseum.is

Húsavík is Iceland's whale-watching capital. There are daily tours between March and December. Do not miss the superb Whale Museum. The coast offers good walks along grassy headlands and little beaches from where you might see seals.

A whale off the coast of Húsavík

8 Lake Mývatn

Whether you have come to this country to climb cinder cones, hike your way over steaming expanses of solidified lava, bathe in open-air geothermal pools, see hot mud pools, make a day-trip into the stark Interior deserts or simply to spend some time bird-watching, you will find it all at Lake Mývatn *(see pp20–21)*. Although many of the sights are located around the lakeshore, you will need a vehicle in order to reach the outlying attractions, which include a flooded volcano crater known as "Hell".

Dettifoss waterfall

9 Dettifoss
MAP F2

The roads to this waterfall *(see p44)* are gravel and open for only a few months each year. The eastern approach is easiest and traverses a stony volcanic plateau, with mountains in the distance. There is a detour well worth taking to Hafragilsfoss, a splendid waterfall just downstream, with a viewpoint inside the Jökulsárgljúfur canyon.

10 Jökulsárgljúfur
MAP F2

Set in a northern segment of the massive Vatnajökull National Park *(see pp24–5)*, this mighty canyon is excellent for hiking, following the top of the gorge or cutting across a land rich in flowers and birdlife. Sights along the way include striking red formations at Rauðhólar, twisted hexagonal basalt columns at Hljóðaklettar, Hólmatungur's springs and Dettifoss *(see p44)*.

A DAY IN THE LAKE MÝVATN AREA

▶ MORNING

Start early, and you can just about pack all of the attractions of **Lake Mývatn** *(see pp20–21)* into one long summer day. Begin with the subterranean hot pools at Grjótagjá, then move south to tackle **Hverfjall's** *(see p21)* slippery black slopes, making a circuit of the rim for spectacular views of the whole Mývatn area. Back at ground level, **Dimmuborgir** *(see p20)* presents an extraordinary maze of natural lava sculptures (look for rare gyrfalcons nesting on rocky towers here), with only a short drive to the lakeshore at Höfði Nature Park, where you will definitely encounter numerous species of waterfowl, including barrow's goldeneye, scaup and mergansers. Follow the road to the south side of the lake at Skútustaðir, home to a large group of grassy pseudocraters.

AFTERNOON

Depending on your progress, you can grab lunch at the Dimmuborgir or Skútustaðir cafés, or circuit the lake to Reykjahlíð's Gamli Bærinn. Head east to the fearsome **Námaskarð** *(see p21)* mud pits, set in a wasteland full of steam and eye-watering smells. A good side road runs north from here, via the Leirbotn Power Station, to where Víti volcano overlooks Leirhnjúkur, a huge expanse of steaming lava laid down in the 1980s – a place for careful exploration. Round off the day with a good soak on the way home at the **Jarðböðin Nature Baths** *(see p21)*.

See map on pp94–5 ←

The Best of the Rest

Goðafoss waterfall

① Goðafoss
This waterfall (see p45) is named after events that occurred when Christianity came here in AD 1000.

② Glaumbær
MAP D2 ■ Glaumbær, 556 Varmahlíð ■ 453 6173 ■ Open mid-May–mid-Sep: 9am–6pm daily; Apr–May & mid-Sep–mid-Oct: 10am–4pm Mon–Fri (by request mid-Oct–Mar: Mon–Fri) ■ Adm ■ www.glaumbaer.is
Classic turf farmhouses built between 1750 and 1879. The use of imported timber hints at the family's comparative wealth.

③ Hofsós
MAP C4
Visit the Icelandic Emigration Centre (see p42), one of the country's oldest timber buildings (Pakkhúsið), and have a dip in the pool (see p53).

④ Vaglaskógur
MAP E2 ■ 462 4755
■ Campsite: open May–Sep
This stretch of birch woodland along Fnjóskadalur valley is a popular camping area with a store and walking trails.

⑤ Laufás
MAP E2 ■ 463 3196 ■ Open May–Oct ■ Adm ■ www.akmus.is
The heritage site and museum, housed in a 19th-century turf farmhouse, displays period household items. The town's church is also worth visiting for its 17th-century pulpit.

⑥ Grenjaðarstaður
MAP E2 ■ 464 3688 ■ Open Jun–Aug 10am–6pm daily ■ Adm
Some buildings here have flowers on their turf roofs. Visit the cemetery to see headstones carved with runes.

⑦ Laxá í Aðaldal
Better known for its fishing potential further downstream, the Laxá's turbulent flow as it exits Lake Mývatn (see p21) is a magnet for red-necked phalarope, barrow's goldeneye and harlequin duck.

⑧ Þingeyrakirkja
MAP C2 ■ Þingeyrar, near Blönduós ■ 895 4473 ■ Open Jun–Aug: 10am–5pm daily ■ Adm
Built between 1864 and 1977, this remarkable church (see p39) sits alone on a vegetated sandbar. A visitor centre next door runs guided tours.

⑨ Hvítserkur
MAP C4
This natural rock formation, which resembles a 15-m- (49-ft-) tall dinosaur drinking from the sea, lies on the east of the Vatnsnes peninsula on Route 711.

Hvítserkur rock formation

⑩ Tjörnes
MAP E2
This rounded peninsula with distinct banded geological strata yields bivalve and plant fossils. A signposted fossil bed is located near Ytri-Tunga farm.

Places to Eat

PRICE CATEGORIES

For a three-course meal for one with half a bottle of wine (or equivalent meal), including taxes and extra charges.

Ⓚ under ISK5,000   ⓀⓀ ISK5,000–9,000
ⓀⓀⓀ over ISK9,000

1 Hótel KEA
MAP E2 ▪ Hafnarstræti 87–89, 600 Akureyri ▪ 460 2000 ▪ ⓀⓀ

The restaurant in Hótel KEA *(see p130)* offers everything from lunch to à la carte dining. Try the Galloway hamburger.

2 Gamli Bærinn
MAP F2 ▪ Reykjahlíð, Mývatn ▪ 464 4170 ▪ Closed Sep–Apr ▪ Ⓚ

This café-bar in Icelandair Hótel Mývatn serves beer, light meals, snacks, coffee and great lamb soup.

3 Hótel Gígur
MAP F3 ▪ Ⓚ

This hotel restaurant *(see p130)* has beautiful views out over the pseudo-craters on Mývatn's southern shore. Serves local fish and lamb.

4 Sjavarborg Restaurant
MAP C3 ▪ Strandgata 1, Hvammstangi ▪ 451 3131 ▪ www.sjavarborg-restaurant.is ▪ ⓀⓀⓀ

Located on Hvammstangi's harbour, this restaurant offers a range of main courses, including, fish soup and fresh fish. Order a cocktail to accompany your meal and leave room for cake.

5 Greifinn
MAP E2 ▪ Glerágata 20, Akureyri ▪ 460 1600 ▪ Ⓚ

A no-nonsense pizza restaurant, with an extensive menu. Takeaway options are available but it is also a lovely place to sit and eat.

6 Bláa Kannan
MAP E2 ▪ Hafnarstræti 96, Akureyri ▪ 461 4600 ▪ Ⓚ

With an unmistakable corrugated iron exterior painted dark blue, and tables spilling out onto the street, this is your best bet in town for coffee, cake and people-watching.

7 Hótel Blanda
MAP D2 ▪ Aðalgata 6, 540 Blönduós ▪ 452 4205 ▪ ⓀⓀ

The restaurant at this hotel offers lunch and dinner menus featuring a range of meat as well as fish dishes prepared with the catch-of-the-day.

8 Gamli Baukur
MAP E2 ▪ Harbour, Húsavík ▪ 464 2442 ▪ Closed mid-Sep–mid-May ▪ Ⓚ

Housed in wooden warehouses overlooking the harbour, this snug place serves soups and fresh fish daily, all at a reasonable cost, given the portions. Limited outdoor seating is available.

9 Salka
MAP E2 ▪ Garðarsbraut 6, Húsavík ▪ 464 2551 ▪ Ⓚ

Offering competition to nearby Gamli Baukur, this restaurant has a similar menu but with the bonus of plenty of outdoor tables to linger at when the sun is shining.

10 Bautinn
MAP E2 ▪ Hafnarstræti 92, Akureyri ▪ 462 1818 ▪ Ⓚ

This unpretentious restaurant has been operating since 1971. It serves a selection of fresh fish, lamb, steaks, pizza and burgers.

Bautinn restaurant

See map on pp94–5

🔟 East Iceland

East Iceland covers a varied region of broad river valleys, boggy plateaus surrounding the Vatnajökull icecap, and a dramatic coastline forming the East Fjords. The main centres are Egilsstaðir, on the shores of Lögurinn lake, and Höfn, a springboard for Vatnajökull National Park. Visiting smaller communities such as Vopnafjörður, Borgarfjörður Eystri and Seyðisfjörður provides insight into daily life here, while rewarding side trips include the Kárahnjúkar hydro dam.

Skriðuklaustur

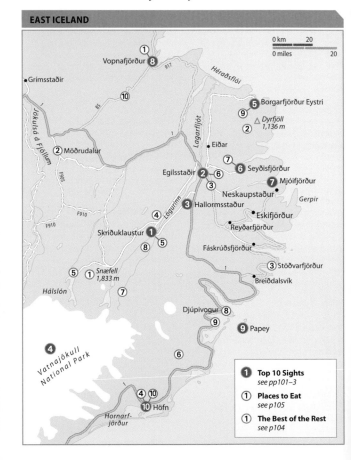

EAST ICELAND

0 km   20
0 miles   20

- Vopnafjörður ⑧
- 917
- Héraðsflói
- Grímsstaðir
- ⑩
- 85
- Jökulsá á Fjöllum
- ② Möðrudalur
- F905
- F910
- F910
- Lagarfljót
- 1
- Eiðar
- ⑤ Borgarfjörður Eystri
- ⑨ △ Dyrfjöll 1,136 m
- ②
- ⑦
- ⑥ Seyðisfjörður
- Egilsstaðir ② ⑥
- ③
- ⑦ Mjóifjörður
- Neskaupstaður
- Gerpir
- ③ Hallormsstaður
- Lögurinn
- ④
- Eskifjörður
- Reyðarfjörður
- Skriðuklaustur ①
- ⑧ ⑤
- Fáskrúðsfjörður
- ⑤ ① Snæfell 1,833 m
- ③ Stöðvarfjörður
- Breiðdalsvík
- Hálslón
- ⑦
- Djúpivogur ⑧
- ⑨
- ⑨ Papey
- ④ Vatnajökull National Park
- ⑥
- ④ ⑩
- ⑩ Höfn
- Hornafjörður

① **Top 10 Sights**
see pp101–3

① **Places to Eat**
see p105

① **The Best of the Rest**
see p104

1 Skriðuklaustur
MAP G3 ▪ 471 2990 ▪ Open
Jun–Aug: 10am–6pm daily; May & Sep:
11am–5pm daily; Apr & Oct: noon–4pm
daily; Nov–Feb: open occasionally, call
in advance ▪ www.skriduklaustur.is

This villa belonging to author Gunnar
Gunnarsson (1889–1975) sits on
Lögurinn's western shore, close to
the church at Valþjófsstaður and
Hengifoss. Gunnarsson's first novel,
Af Borgslægtens Historie, was filmed
here. The villa hosts exhibitions
about the author and the ruins of a
16th century monastery found nearby.
Klausturkaffi offers lunch and a buffet
of homemade cakes. The Visitor Centre
for Vatnajökull National Park is
located nearby in a separate building.

2 Egilsstaðir
MAP G3 ▪ Summer-only buses
from Akureyri and Reykjavík via Höfn;
airport open year-round ▪ East Iceland
Heritage Museum: check website for
opening times; www.minjasafn.is/
english; adm ▪ Wilderness Center:
www.wilderness.is

Just east of Lögurinn lake, Egilsstaðir's
attractions include the East Iceland
Heritage Museum, which features
a *baðstofa* (the living room of a turf
house) and the Wilderness Center –
a guesthouse within a museum
celebrating how Icelanders have
survived in this difficult environment. The 70-km (44-mile) drive
around Lögurinn takes in saga
sites, woodlands and one of
Iceland's tallest waterfalls.

Hallormsstaður forest

3 Hallormsstaður
MAP G3

Hallormsstaður sits beside Iceland's
most extensive forest, grown since
the 1900s for recreational use and
for timber. A web of wooded walking
trails heads up the valley slopes,
while a roadside Forestry Office has
a small arboretum with 40 tree
species, including Iceland's tallest,
a 22-m- (62-ft-) high larch.

4 Vatnajökull National Park
MAP F4

The bulk of Europe's largest national
park surrounds the Vatnajökull
(see pp24–5) icecap, whose fringes
are 100 km (62 miles) southwest
of Egilsstaðir or 10 km (6 miles)
northwest of Höfn. In the vicinity
of Skaftafell and Höfn, and easily
accessible from the ring road, various
glacier outlets crawl down to the low-
land. Lakes have formed in front of
most of these ice tongues making
them especially picturesque. Various
activities, such as glacier walks and
snowmobile tours are offered in the
area south of Vatnajökull.

Vatnajökull icecap, seen from Jökulsárlón lake

Borgafjörður Eystri settlement

5 Borgafjörður Eystri (Bakkagerði)
MAP H2

Part of the fun of visiting Borgafjörður Eystri, the East Fjords' most endearing settlement, is the journey via the Héraðsflói estuary's grassy lagoons and steep ranges that isolate the village. On arrival you will find a tiny community backed by the jagged Dyrfjöll mountain, with sights including a little hummock near the church named Álfaborg, home to Iceland's fairy queen (according to folklore), and a sizable puffin colony overlooking the fishing harbour. Superb, lengthy hiking trails lead south to Seyðisfjörður.

6 Seyðisfjörður
MAP H3

Seyðisfjörður's charm lies in its steep fjord setting and 19th-century wooden architecture near the harbour. The church, several houses and two hotels are the pick, most painted in pastel hues and originally imported from Norway. An important naval station during World War II and a herring port before then, today Seyðisfjörður is linked to the Faroe Islands and Denmark by the *Norröna* ferry.

7 Mjóifjörður
MAP H3

A long, thin inlet accessed by the gravel Route 953, Mjóifjörður ("Narrow Fjord") is worth the bumpy drive to Brekka village and the remote lighthouse at Dalatangi. The road between the shoreline and steep mountains offers some close-ups of beautiful streams and cascades, plus the chance of seeing the Arctic fox, which is more at ease with humans in this remote area.

8 Vopnafjörður
MAP G2

If you are making the long coastal drive along Route 85 from Húsavík towards Egilsstaðir, set aside an hour for Vopnafjörður, a small town built on a steep prong of land. It has a museum detailing the plight of local communities following the 1875 eruption of Víti at Askja *(see p47)*. An outdoor geothermal pool at Selárdalur and the immaculate collection of old turf farmhouses at Bustarfell *(see p104)* are located close by.

19th-century architecture, Seyðisfjörður

9 Papey
MAP H4

Papey is one of the highlights of East Iceland, featuring rock ledges full of snoozing seals and seabirds. This small, grass-topped island is thought to have been inhabited by monks before the Vikings arrived *(see p71)*. Often due to a lack of captains there are no ferries to this island.

Lighthouse on Papey island

10 Höfn
MAP G5 ■ **Year-round buses to Reykjavík and summer services to Egilsstaðir; airport open year-round**

Höfn started life as a warehouse during the 1860s, and developed into a working port. It is a good base for trips to Vatnajökull National Park *(see pp24–5)*. The Glacier Exhibition fills you in on the area and you can book Skidoo trips and Jeep tours to the icecap. Hikers can aim for Lónsöræfi reserve. For glacier views, head for the landmark statue on the shore – avoiding the Arctic tern colony

HÉRAÐSFLÓI'S BIRDLIFE

Héraðsflói – a broad bay with a black-sand beach and boggy meadows inland along the myriad of streamlets of the Jökulsá á Brú river – makes a superb place for observing birdlife. Look for marine ducks (including the long-tailed or old squaw and scoter), godwits, red-throated divers and even hobbys, Iceland's smallest bird of prey.

A DAY IN EAST ICELAND

▶ MORNING

Before starting this 70-km (44-mile) circuit of Lögurinn lake and the Lagarfljót valley, climb the hillock behind the Menntaskólinn school in Egilsstaðir *(see p101)* for a view of the region – on a clear day you can see as far as Snæfell *(see p104)*, Iceland's highest free-standing peak. Then head south, branching off the highway onto Route 931, past fields full of sheep and Icelandic horses, until a surprising amount of woodland begins to spring up around Hallormsstaður *(see p101)*, where you can explore walking tracks or the Forestry Office's arboretum, or take in lakeside views at Atlavík. Exiting the woods past Atlavík, the main road crosses the lake to Lögurinn's west shore, where you turn left and drive some distance to Skriðuklaustur *(see p101)*.

AFTERNOON

After having a snack at Skriðuklaustur's café, Klausturkaffi, and visiting the National Park exhibition, continue south to Valþófsstaður church *(see p104)* with its reproduction of carved Viking doors, then retrace your route back past Skriðuklaustur to where the 60-km- (37-mile-) long Route 910 ascends to moorlands around Snæfell and the Kárahnjúkar Hydro Dam *(see p104)*. You need 3 hours for this round trip, otherwise follow an hour-long walking track uphill to Hengifoss *(see p104)* after parking your car. Stay on the western shore for the drive back to Egilsstaðir.

See map on p100 ←

The Best of the Rest

1 Snæfell
MAP F4 ▪ www.vatnajokulsth jodgardur.is

This isolated, snowcapped basalt core of an old volcano lies at Vatnajökull's northeast corner. It is located on a 4WD-only track. There are hiking huts around the base.

2 Hvítserkur
MAP H3

Spectacular orange, pink and grey rhyolite mountain 10 km (6 miles) along a hiking trail from Borgafjörður Eystri. The colours really stand out after rain. The trail is straight-forward, but be prepared for changing weather.

3 Steinasafn Petru
MAP H4 ▪ Fjarðarbraut 21, 755 Stöðvarfirði, East Fjords ▪ 475 8834 ▪ Open May–Sep/Oct: 9am–6pm daily ▪ Adm

Extensive private geological collection, featuring coloured stones, crystals and mineral samples found in mainly the eastern part of Iceland.

4 Hengifoss
MAP G3

This 118-m (387-ft) waterfall is Iceland's highest, dropping in a narrow ribbon off a cliff face lay-ered in red and black. On the way up, don't miss the twisted basalt columns at Litlifoss.

5 Kárahnjúkar Hydro Dam
MAP F4

A controversial project that dammed the Dimmugljúfur canyon in order to provide power for a smelter. The sealed road crosses highland tundra, which is home to reindeer.

6 Lónsöræfi
MAP G4

This wild, uninhabited area is rich in gorges, moorland and glacial scenery. An unmarked, 5-day trail for self-sufficient hikers runs from Stafafell to Snæfell through this private reserve.

7 Eyjabakkar
MAP G4

Boggy highland region en route to Kárahnjúkar or Snæfell, this is a breeding ground for greylag geese and whooper swans; reindeer are common too.

8 Valþjófsstaður
MAP G3 ▪ Open 10am–5pm daily

Farm and red-roofed church, with replica carved doors depicting a knight slaying a dragon. The original doors, dating from around AD 1200, are in Reykjavík's National Museum.

9 Djúpivogur Bulandsnes
MAP G4 ▪ www.djupivogur.is

Three beautiful fjords and a profusion of Icelandic wildlife make this area a nature-lover's paradise.

10 Bustarfell
MAP G2 ▪ 471 2211 ▪ Open 10 Jun–20 Sep 10am–5pm daily ▪ Adm

Well-preserved turf-roofed farm-houses (rebuilt in 1770), occupied by the same family since 1532. Café on site.

Hengifoss

Places to Eat

PRICE CATEGORIES

For a three-course meal for one with half a bottle of wine (or equivalent meal), including taxes and extra charges.

Ⓚ under ISK5,000 ⓀⓀ ISK5,000–9,000
ⓀⓀⓀ over ISK9,000

1 Hótel Tangi

MAP G2 ■ Hafnarbyggð 17, Vopnafjörður ■ 473 1203 ■ ⓀⓀ

The hotel restaurant is the most popular place to eat in Vopnafjörður, and it's not hard to see why as their pizzas and grilled fish are excellent.

2 Fjallakaffi

MAP F3 ■ Möðrudal á Fjöllum ■ 471 1858, 894 0758 ■ www.fjalladyrd.is ■ Ⓚ

Attached to the highest farm in Iceland (which offers accommodation), this "café in the mountains" is reached by Route 901, south off Route 1 from Lake Mývatn. Fjallakaffi serves traditional fare, including *kjötsúpa* (lamb soup), *sláturterta* (lamb tart) and *kleina* (an Icelandic doughnut).

3 Icelandair Hótel Hérað

MAP G3 ■ Miðvangur 5–7, 700 Egilsstaðir ■ 471 1500 ■ Ⓚ

Local reindeer steak is the obvious dish to try at the restaurant in Hérað *(see p130)*. They also offer lamb and seafood dishes.

4 Humarhöfnin

MAP G5 ■ Hafnarbraut 4, Höfn ■ 478 1200 ■ www.humarhofnin.is ■ ⓀⓀ

Look for this restaurant's distinctive orange-and-white exterior on the harbour in Höfn, and prepare to demolish its signature grilled langoustine tails in garlic, butter and parsley.

5 Klausturkaffi

MAP G3 ■ Skriðuklaustur ■ 471 2992 ■ Open Apr–mid-Oct ■ ⓀⓀ

This charming café serves Icelandic staples as well as a delicious lunch and cake buffet everyday in summer.

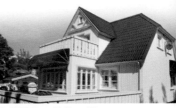

Café Nielsen, Egilsstaðir

6 Café Nielsen

MAP G3 ■ Tjarnarbraut 1, Egilsstaðir ■ 471 2626 ■ ⓀⓀ

This restaurant-bar is housed in a wooden building with an outdoor deck. The fillet of lamb with wild thyme, gravy and baked potato is excellent. Try the reasonable lunch buffets.

7 Nordic

MAP H3 ■ Norðurgata 2, 710 Seyðisfjörður ■ 472 1277 ■ Ⓚ

This restaurant in Hótel Aldan *(see p132)* is great for a three-course meal. They also offer fish and chips.

8 Hótel Framtið

MAP G4 ■ Vogaland 4, 765 Djúpivogur ■ 478 8887 ■ ⓀⓀ

Fill up on hearty fish dishes and roast lamb fillet with thyme sauce at this eatery in Hótel Framtið *(see p130)* on Djúpivogur's harbour before making the trip over to Papey island.

9 Álfacafé

MAP H2 ■ Borgafjörður Eystri ■ 862 9802, 472 9900 ■ Ⓚ

Housed inside a former fish factory near Borgafjörður Eystri's old harbour, Álfacafé has exceptionally heavy tables and crockery made out of solid stone. Only light meals are served and the sandwiches are good.

10 Pakkhús

MAP G5 ■ Krosseyjarvegi 3, 780 Höfn í Hornafirði ■ 478 2280 ■ Closed mid-Dec–mid-Jan ■ www.pakkhus.is ■ ⓀⓀ

The wonderful Pakkhús *(see p62)* has the perfect ambience for their special langoustine by the harbour.

See map on p100

TOP 10 South Iceland

South Iceland has a rich band of coastline, minor icecaps, fertile river plains and explosive volcanic landscapes, all wrapped up in history and folklore. The Blue Lagoon and the "Golden Circle", which includes Þingvellir, Geysir and Gullfoss, are Iceland's most iconic sights. There is also the Hekla volcano, a wealth of saga locations, waterfalls, hiking grounds, the gem-like Westman Islands and peaceful Vík village, all in easy reach of Reykjavík. You will need more time to reach Kirkjubæjarklaustur town, the Jökulsárlón glacial lagoon and the fringes of Vatnajökull National Park.

The Blue Lagoon

1 Þingvellir National Park

This amazing rift valley (see pp12–13), now a UNESCO World Heritage site, was the setting for Iceland's open-air parliament in Viking times. Stop at the Visitor Centre on the way along Route 36 for superlative views over the rift walls and the lava plains. Pick out key features such as the Law Rock, Þingvellir Church, Almannagjá canyon, Öxarárfoss waterfall, Þingvallavatn lake and the Skjaldbreiður volcano.

Öxará river, Þingvellir National Park

SOUTH ICELAND

Faxaflói

Skorradalsvatn

Miðsandur

Akranes

Þingvellir National Park ①

② Gullfoss

③ Geysir

Reykjavík ⑩

Skálholt

⑥ Flúðir

Þórisv

Hafnarfjörður

Hveragerði ⑦

⑤ Þjórsárdalur

Ljótipollu

Keflavík ⑨

Selfoss ②

Hella

⑤

△ Hekla 1,491 m

⑥ ④

Eyrarbakki

⑦ ⑧

⑦ ⑧ ⑩

⑧ ⑨

Fljótshlíð ⑥

Blue Lagoon

Hvolsvöllur

① △ Katla 1,250 m

③ Skógar

Landeyjahöfn

Vestmannaeyjar ⑦

Heimaey

⑧ Vík

0 kilometres 40

0 miles 40

Surtsey

Previous pages Kirkjugólf ("The Church Floor"), Kirkjubæjarklaustur

Gullfoss, Iceland's most dramatic waterfall

2 Gullfoss

The final stop on a tour of the "Golden Circle", Gullfoss (see pp18–19) is Iceland's most dramatic waterfall and it is deafening, except in winter. Make sure you get a look at it from as many viewpoints as possible – especially from the top of the canyon, where you can appreciate the Hvítá river's journey from the barren Interior to the north.

3 Geysir

It is incredible to find such a raw, primal sight as Geysir's scalding waterspouts erupting by the side of the main road. Just 90 minutes from the capital, Geysir has a hotel, petrol station and tourist centre. The key geyser to watch is Strokkur, which erupts every few minutes (you would be very lucky to see the original vent, Geysir itself, blow its top, as it is very rare now). The whole site (see pp16–17) is surrounded by a collection of smaller hot pools, each with its own distinct character.

4 The Blue Lagoon

Iceland's southwest extreme, the Reykjanes peninsula, is almost entirely covered in barren lava fields, which makes finding the vivid Blue Lagoon (see pp14–15) hidden within it doubly surprising. Making creative use of waste water from a geothermal power plant, the Blue Lagoon offers an outstanding experience of outdoor soaking. Its white silt is said to have health benefits, too.

5 Þjórsárdalur

MAP D5 ■ Both access roads subject to closure ■ Þjóðveldisbærinn: Open Jun–Aug: 10am–6pm daily; www.thjodveldisbaer.is ■ Þjórsárdalslaug: see www.swimminginiceland.com for latest information ■ Adm

Þjórsárdalur is a broad, stark river valley, which was shaped by an eruption in 1102 of the Hekla volcano (see p46), just one ridge away to the east. The eruption buried a Viking longhouse up the valley at Stöng, which has now been excavated and is open to the public, reached via a gravel track, with a full reconstruction nearby at Þjóðveldisbærinn. There is a swimming pool in the small village of Árnes, next to the Þjórsárstofa visitor centre.

Hamarinn 1,579 m

Grímsvötn 1,719 m

Vatnajökull

Skaftafell

Jökulsárlón 10

Lómagnúpur

irkjubæjarklaustur

Fagurhólsmýri

9

6 Fljótshlíð

MAP D5 ■ Saga Centre: open Jun–mid-Sep: 9am–6pm daily; adm; www.njala.is

To reach the Markarfljót valley, take Route 1 to Hvolsvöllur township – where you should visit the excellent Saga Centre – and then follow the 30-km- (19-mile-) long Route 261 east. The area is central to key scenes from *Njál's Saga*, including the farm Völlur, where the tale opens, and Hlíðarendi, home to the virtuous Gunnar Hámundarson. There is a church on the hillside at Hlíðarendi today, from which you can look seawards over the valley, where landmarks like rocky Stóri-Dímon stand proud.

NJÁL'S SAGA

This saga is a gripping account of a bloody, 50-year-long family feud revolving around the household of Njáll Þorgeirsson, in which the evil scheming of Mörð Valgarðsson causes the deaths of both Njáll and his friend Gunnar Hámundarson. The hard-boiled delivery is softened by deadpan humour and vivid insights into daily life during Viking times.

7 Vestmannaeyjar

MAP C6 ■ Daily ferry from Landeyjahöfn (from Þorlákshöfn in bad weather), flights from Reykjavík and Bakki

The Westman Islands are a string of volcanic outcrops off the south coast, which include the world's newest island, Surtsey. Heimaey, the largest and only inhabited island in the group, is famous for the 1973 Eldfell eruption, which partially buried Heimaey town and almost ended its fishing industry. Visitors can climb Eldfell's still-steaming slopes or walk around the coast in half a day. The museum Eldheimar (www. eldheimar.is) has exhibits on the Heimaey and Surtsey eruptions. Another highlight is the annual Þjóðhátíð festival (see p68) held here.

8 Vík

MAP D6

This peaceful seafront community of around 300 people is located below Reynisfjall's cliffs, Vík boasts a dramatic black-sand beach, great views east over the flat Mýrdalssandur black-lava desert, lively bird colonies and some towering offshore black stacks known as the Troll Rocks. Skógar and its waterfall, Skógafoss (see p45) are 30 minutes up the road and there are more seascapes to be

View from the top of Eldfell volcano, Vestmannaeyjar

enjoyed to the west at Reynisfjall and Dyrhólaey (see p50). Also close by are a number of walking tracks.

9 Kirkjubæjarklaustur
MAP E5

A tiny highway town in the middle of nowhere, Kirkjubæjarklaustur is surrounded by pseudocraters and hexagonal lava pavements known as Kirkjugólf ("The Church Floor"), with summer access to the awesome Lakagígar craters (see p46). The town's name – literally Church Farm Monastery – reflects its origins in 1186 as a convent. Moving east, Skaftafell in Vatnajökull National Park (see pp24–5) is an hour's drive away, on the other side of the black, sandy Skeiðarársandur desert.

Icebergs at Jökulsárlón

10 Jökulsárlón
MAP G5

This is an essential stop on the long journey between Vík and Höfn. The icebergs, glacier tongue and rushing waters of Jökulsárlón – not to mention the bizarre sight of ice boulders on the beach – break the monotony of the bleak expanses of black gravel along the coastal fringes (see pp32–3). Seals are the pick of the wildlife commonly encountered here, although there is also plenty of birdlife to look out for. Lagoon cruises lasting about half an hour are an option during the summer months.

A DAY IN SOUTH ICELAND

MORNING

Begin a classic "Golden Circle" tour by heading northeast from Reykjavík up Route 36, looking out along the way for the boxy, two-storey white house of the late author and Nobel Laureate Halldór Laxness. After passing Þingvallavatn's blue expanse you arrive on the west side of the Þingvellir rift valley (see pp12–13), where it is time to spend an hour – or the entire day – soaking up the history and landscapes at Iceland's cultural heart. Cross the rift and take Route 365 to Laugarvatn (see p59), where you could stop and have a swim at the National School for Sports, before pressing further along Routes 37 and 35 to spectacular water features at Geysir (see pp16–17) and Gullfoss (see pp18–19).

AFTERNOON

Have lunch at either Hótel Geysir (see p113), where you can get a proper three-course meal, or at Gullfoss' Visitor Centre, whose café does excellent lamb soup. Then follow Route 35 southwest to Skálholt (see p39), a bishopric and educational centre since the 11th century. Route 35 continues southwest from Skálholt past the Kerið crater (see p112) to Selfoss, a busy town on the Ölfusá river, where the bridge was the cause of Iceland's first strike. The highway runs straight back to Reykjavík via the greenhouses at Hveragerði (famous for its flowers and vegetables), or you can detour coastwards to the villages of Stokkseyri and Eyrarbakki (see p112).

See map on pp108–9

The Best of the Rest

1 Mýrdalsjökull
MAP D6 ▪ www.mountain guides.is ▪ www.arcanum.is

This icecap conceals the dangerous Katla volcano (see p47). The lowest glacier tongue, Sólheimajökull, is accessible off Route 1. Here, you can hike the glacier or ride a snowmobile.

2 Kerið
MAP C5

This deep but small crater north of Selfoss is best viewed on a sunny day to appreciate the red and black slopes contrasting with the water.

3 Seljavallalaug
MAP D6 ▪ Seljavellir

Soak among wild scenery below the site of the 2010 Eyjafjallajökull eruption in this open-air thermal pool, tucked away at the end of a rough walking track.

4 Inside the Volcano
MAP C5 ▪ Open mid-May–mid-Oct ▪ Tour duration: 5–6 hours ▪ Adm ▪ www.insidethevolcano.com

Be lowered in an open-sided cage 120 m (390 ft) into the huge magma chamber of an extinct volcano for a fascinating experience.

5 Leirubakki
MAP D5 ▪ Route 26 ▪ 487 8700 ▪ Summer buses between Reykjavík and Landmannalaugar ▪ www.leirubakki.is

Farm and hotel near Mount Hekla (see p31), with a volcano museum and a lava-block hot tub with views of the mountain.

6 Bridge Between Continents
MAP C5

The European and American continental plates separate visibly at Þingvellir – cross between them on this bridge, a 20-minute drive from the Blue Lagoon or Keflavík.

7 Hveragerði
MAP C5

Hveragerði (see p55) is Iceland's major greenhouse town, using geothermal heat to grow flowers and vegetables on a commercial scale. There are hiking trails and a swimming pool.

8 Hvolsvöllur Saga Centre
MAP C6 ▪ Hlíðarvegur 14, Hvolsvöllur ▪ 487 8781 ▪ Open summer: 11:30am–11pm daily; winter: 10am–5pm Sat & Sun ▪ Adm ▪ www.njala.is

Lively exhibition dedicated to the Viking era and the world of sagas.

9 Lava Centre
MAP C6 ▪ Hvolsvöllur ▪ 415 5200 ▪ Open 9am–7pm daily (restaurant open till 9pm) ▪ Adm ▪ www.lavacentre.is

This interactive and impressively high-tech exhibition explores the country's geologic activity, from volcano explosions and earthquakes to glacial floods. There is also a decent restaurant on site.

10 Stokkseyri and Eyrarbakki
MAP C5 ▪ www.husid.com

Delightful villages with great seafood restaurants and the Húsið museum.

The Inside the Volcano tour

Places to Eat

PRICE CATEGORIES
For a three-course meal for one with half a bottle of wine (or equivalent meal), including taxes and extra charges.
....
Ⓚ under ISK5,000   ⓀⓀ ISK5,000–9,000
ⓀⓀⓀ over ISK9,000

1 Hótel Rangá
MAP C5 ■ Ringroad, near Hella ■ 487 5700 ■ ⓀⓀ

Nordic-European cuisine is served at this splendid hotel restaurant (see p131) with views of the finest salmon river in Iceland. Be sure to try the signature dish – salmon sous-vide.

2 Krisp
MAP C5 ■ Eyravegur 8, Selfoss ■ 482 4099 ■ Ⓚ

Local cuisine presented with an Asian twist. Great salads and steaks.

3 Hótel Geysir
MAP C5 ■ Haukadalur, Geysir ■ 480 6800 ■ ⓀⓀ

Generous breakfast and lunch buffets, an à la carte dinner menu and great views of the Geysir area make this hotel-restaurant (see p17) the best place to eat in the area.

4 Hótel Selfoss
MAP C5 ■ Eyravegur 2, Selfoss ■ 480 2500 ■ ⓀⓀ

This up-market option serves a well-presented menu of Icelandic seafood and meat staples.

5 Gullfoss Kaffi
MAP D4 ■ Gullfoss ■ 486 6500 ■ Ⓚ

With wide vistas of the surrounding landscape – though not of Gullfoss itself – this spacious, wooden-framed café is a great spot to pull up for a bowl of lamb soup.

6 Hótel Flúðir
MAP C5 ■ Vesturbrún 1, Flúðir ■ 486 6630 ■ ⓀⓀ

Isolated modern building on the edge of a farming town, Hótel Flúðir has splendid views and a menu featuring locally grown greenhouse vegetables and native meats.

7 Rauða Húsið
MAP C5 ■ Búðarstíg 4, Eyrarbakki ■ 483 3330 ■ ⓀⓀ

A good reason to visit the charming Eyrarbakki village, this restaurant in a historic house offers splendid lobster, lamb and fish dishes at a fraction of their cost in Reykjavík.

Lobster dish at Rauða Húsið

8 Hafið Bláa
MAP C5 ■ Þorlákshöfn, near Óseyrar Bridge, Eyrarbakki ■ 483 1000 ■ Ⓚ

With stunning surround views, this is another excellent dining experience at the mouth of the Ölfusá river. The menu is dominated by an exceptional selection of lobster and fish dishes.

9 Kaffi Duus
MAP B5 ■ Duusgata 10, Keflavík ■ 421 7080 ■ ⓀⓀ

This smart place is not far from the Keflavík International Airport, which makes it an ideal location to tuck into tasty lamb, lobster and salmon dishes before heading homewards.

10 Fjöruborðið
MAP C5 ■ Eyrarbraut 3a, 825 Stokkseyri ■ 483 1550 ■ www. fjorubordid.is ■ ⓀⓀ

Located in the village of Stokkseyri, this restaurant (see p63) features an elaborate food and drinks menu with separate meal options for kids.

See map on pp108–9 ⬅

🔟 The Highland Interior

Inland from the relatively fertile coastline is Iceland's Highland Interior. This is a beautiful wilderness of black gravel, lava plains and glaciated peaks that have been blasted by summer storms and winter frosts. Not surprisingly, the Interior is uninhabited, but the ghosts of numerous pack-horse trails have now been graded for 4WDs only.

Icelandic horse, Hekla

Open for a few weeks in summer, the most accessible of these routes are the Kjölur (from Gullfoss to near Akureyri) and Fjallabak (from Hella to Kirkjubæjarklaustur). Long-distance buses follow these routes from June to September.

THE HIGHLAND INTERIOR

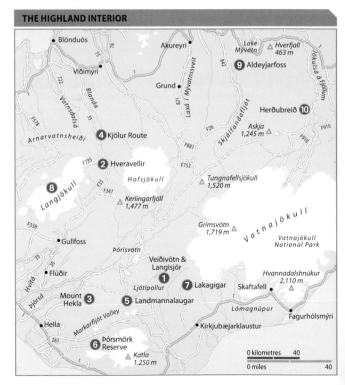

Panoramic view of the spectacular Langisjór lake

1 Veiðivötn and Langisjór
MAP E5

Veiðivötn and Langisjór are part of a complex of inland waterways inside volcanic "stretch marks" southwest of Vatnajökull *(see p24)*, reached off the F208 Fjallabak Route. There are good fishing areas amidst the stark countryside. Veiðivötn is an area of tarns and streams, while Langisjór is a narrow stretch of water. Both are accessible only along rough tracks and there is no public transport.

2 Hveravellir
MAP D4 ■ Summer buses from Reykjavík and Akureyri ■ Bus schedules: www.bsi.is

Halfway along the Kjölur Route, Hveravellir is a desolate hot springs area with an outdoor hot tub, calcified mounds bubbling boiling water, a strong smell of sulphur and a basic hut with bunk beds run by the Icelandic Touring Association *(www.fi.is)*.

3 Mount Hekla

East of Þjórsá river is Mount Hekla *(see p31)*, which means "hooded", after the clouds that obscure its summit. It was once believed to be the entrance to hell, due to its eruptions followed by months of noisy "grumbling" (taken to be the sound of tormented souls). On a good day, you can see the mountain from Hella on Route 1, and you will pass close to it en route to Landmannalaugar. Many companies run 4WD circuits and trips to the mountain in summer.

4 The Kjölur Route
MAP D4 ■ Bus schedule: www.bsi.is ■ Road open mid-Jun–late Aug

The Kjölur Route (Kjalvegur) is the least difficult of the Highland roads to traverse, running for 170 km (106 miles) from Gullfoss *(see pp18–19)* to Route 1 near Blönduós *(see p95)*. All the major rivers have been bridged and the gravel track is safe for cars. Sights along the way include Hveravellir's hot springs and the Langjökull icecap.

5 Landmannalaugar
MAP D5

Relatively accessible and just 3 or 4 hours' drive from Reykjavík, Landmannalaugar delivers a full-on Highland experience. The road takes in volcanic wastelands, exciting river crossings, mountains and hot springs. There are enough hills, lava fields and lakes to spend a day exploring. You could even stay at the bunkhouse or the campsite and spend 4 days hiking to Þórsmörk along the Laugavegur trail *(see p55)*.

Laugavegur hiking trail

6 Þórsmörk Reserve

MAP D6 ▪ Daily buses from Reykjavík ▪ Only accessible mid-Jun–Aug

Iceland's most popular hiking area (see p55), accessible only by 4WD from the highway near Hvolsvöllur via the 30-km- (19-mile-) long F249 – watch out for the potentially dangerous river crossing at the end – or by trekking in along Laugavegur or from Skógar via Fimmvörðuháls (see p54). Set in an exceptionally pretty glacial valley, the pick of the views at Þórsmörk are from Valahnúkur (an easy and short ascent) and Utigönguhöfði (an arduous and long ascent).

7 Lakagígar

MAP E5 ▪ Buses: Jun–Aug daily ▪ Bus schedule: www.bsi.is

This 25-km- (16-mile-) long row of craters erupted with a vengeance in 1783 (see p25), disrupting wea-ther patterns all across Europe and nearly depopulating Iceland. Walking trails ranging in length between 20 minutes and 2 hours allow you to explore the line of cones and expansive lava fields, which are now partly buried under a thick matting of moss and heather. There is no accommodation on site, but mountain huts and campsites can be found along the road. Seasonal

> **HIGHLAND DRIVING**
>
> Rough conditions, no settlements and nobody to help if something goes wrong all make it imperative that Highland roads are tackled only in high-clearance 4WD vehicles. Travel in convoy, check road conditions before setting out (www.vegagerdin.is) and give your route and estimated arrival time to someone reliable so rescue can be organized if needed.

buses from Skaftafell run here via Kirkjubæjarklaustur and the 60-km- (37-mile-) long F206.

8 Langjökull

MAP D4 ▪ Year-round Jeep tours from Reykjavík ▪ www.adventures.is

Iceland's second largest icecap, the "Long Glacier" west of the Kjölur Route, feeds Hvítárvatn and Sandvatn lakes, which in turn drain into the Hvítá river, on which the spectacular Gullfoss waterfalls are located (see pp18–19). There is talk of damming another of Langjökull's lakes, Hagavatn, for hydropower. Apart from seeing the glacier from the Kjölur or Kaldidalur routes, tours run up here for snowmobiling trips – you only get an hour but it is an exhilarating experience, like riding a Jet Ski on snow.

Langjökull, Iceland's second largest icecap

9 Aldeyjarfoss
MAP E3 ■ **Bus schedule:** www.re.is

Although this impressive waterfall on the Skjálfandafljót river sits at the northern end of the otherwise difficult Sprengisandur Route, it is actually located on a good gravel road 30 km (19 miles) south of the Goðafoss waterfall (see p45). Most vehicles can make it with care during the summer, but check conditions first. The surrounding rock formations are what make Aldeyjarfoss so striking. A layer of outlandishly fashioned basalt columns is capped by a thick blanket of solidified lava. Buses negotiating the Sprengisandur crossing between Reykjavík and Akureyri make it a point to stop here.

Basalt columns at Aldeyjarfoss

10 Herðubreið
MAP F3

Widely known as the "Queen of the Icelandic Mountains", Herðubreið's spiky palagonite heights rise to an 1,682 m (5,518 ft) northeast of Askja (see p21), above the dismal Ódáðahraun ("Desert of Evil Deeds"). The slopes are laced with short freshwater springs and covered with the pink blooms of the Arctic river beauty flower in July. You get good views of the mountain on a clear day from the road to Kárahnjúkar in Eyjabakkar (see p104), but if you fancy hiking, stop on the F88 between Mývatn and Askja (see pp20–21).

A DAY IN THE HIGHLANDS

▶ MORNING

Start early for this day trip to **Landmannalaugar** (see p115) and bring a packed lunch. The journey will take upwards of 8 hours, depending on how many times you stop along the way. Head east along Route 1 from Reykjavík via Selfoss and Hella, then turn north up Route 264 to see the Viking buildings at Keldur Farm. With **Mount Hekla** (see p115) looming behind, take a moment to appreciate Keldur's location – so close to an active volcano. Retrace the route towards Hella, then turn north along Route 268 for a half-hour run through lava fields to Mount Hekla and the intersection with Route 26. You could turn left here to **Leirubakki** (see p112), but for Landmannalaugar turn right, driving across the yellow pumice plain between Hekla and the Þjórsá river, before reaching the junction with F225, which heads east to Landmannalaugar. Pull up and enjoy your picnic lunch.

AFTERNOON

The F225 road traverses the black-sand wasteland of Hekla's northern foothills, with several river crossings before it reaches an intersection about 47 km (29 miles). Turn right (south) at this junction, which leads down to **Frostastaðavatn's** (see p31) lakeshore and then right again onto the 5-km- (3-mile-) long F224, which crosses a double fjord before reaching Landmannalaugar. Soak in the spring and then prepare to head back. Once you are on Route 26, simply follow it south to back to Route 1 between the towns of Hella and Selfoss.

See map on p114 ←

Streetsmart

Mount Esja dominating the
Reykjavík skyline

Getting To and Around Iceland

Arriving by Air

Most flights from Europe, the USA and Canada land at **Keflavík International Airport**, 50 km (31 miles) from Reykjavík. The national carrier is **Icelandair**, but you may get better deals with budget operators like **WOW Air**. It takes about 3 hours to reach Iceland from Europe and 5–6 hours from the USA. The cheapest way into town from Keflavík is the **Flybus**, which delivers arrivals to the **BSÍ** long-distance bus station and major hotels in Reykjavík in about 45 mins. Taxis are expensive, but you can arrange to collect rental cars at the airport.

Some flights from Greenland and the Faroe Islands use **Reykjavík International Airport**, just west of the city centre.

Reykjavík International Airport also offers direct domestic flights with **Air Iceland Connect** and **Eagle Air** to Akureyri, Egilsstaðir, Húsavík, the Westman Islands, Ísafjörður, Höfn, Sauðárkrókur, Gjögur and Bíldudalur. From Akureyri, there are connections to Grímsey, Vopnafjörður and Thorshöfn. Both airlines offer day trips and adventure tours. Regional airports generally stay open in winter, when roads might be closed.

Arriving by Sea

From April until the end of October, the **Smyril Line** runs a weekly passenger and vehicle ferry between Denmark and Seyðisfjörður in eastern Iceland. It costs more than flying, and the 3-day crossing can be rough, but you get the chance to visit the Faroe Islands en route and it's the only way to bring your own vehicle into Iceland. International cruise boats also visit Iceland during the summer, docking at Reykjavík, Akureyri, Ísafjörður and Seyðisfjörður.

Travelling by Bus

Strætó serves North and East Iceland as well as Reykjavík and its suburbs as far as Selfoss, Akranes and Hafnarfjörður (7am–midnight Mon–Sat, noon–midnight Sun). The flat fare is ISK350 (you pay the exact amount when boarding), but day and multi-day discount cards are available at the Mjóddin bus station.

From the BSÍ station, **Reykjavík Excursions** run day tours in the south and west of Iceland. During the summer they run the Iceland On Your Own bus services in cooperation with **SBA-Norðurleið**, serving most of Iceland. Similar operators include **Sterna Travel** and **TREX** in Reykjavík. Other parts of the country are covered by local operators. While most destinations are served daily in summer, all Interior services, even those along the Ringroad between Höfn and Egilsstaðir, stop or are reduced at other times.

Passes that restrict you to a specific route and schedule are the more economical than paying for separate journeys. Book bus seats at least a day in advance.

Travelling by Car

You can bring your car to Iceland on the Smyril Line ferry from Denmark. There are car-rental agencies, such as **Iceland Car Rental**, though rates are high. The minimum age for renting a car is 20 (25 for Jeeps). Rental cars might not be insured for some routes. Seatbelts are compulsory and headlights must always be on. Driving is on the right-hand side. Speed limits are 90 kmph (56 mph) on asphalt roads, 80 kmph (50 mph) on gravel roads and 30 kmph (19 mph) in residential areas. Drink-driving and driving off marked roads or tracks are illegal.

Reykjavík's main roads can become gridlocked during rush hour (7:45–9am and 4–6:30pm). Route 1, or the Ringroad, runs a circuit 1,300 km (808 miles) around the country, but it is narrow. Many country roads are unsealed gravel and not suited to fast driving. Roads marked on a map with an F require 4WD at all times. Bad weather can make any road dangerous for conventional vehicles. Many 4WD routes cross dangerous rivers, snowfields and sands, and are suitable for experienced drivers only. Some car-rental agencies offer GPS rental. **Road Conditions** updates information daily about the road conditions and the weather.

Travelling by Taxi

Taxis in Iceland are metered and have uniform fares. There is no tipping. Look for ranks outside major hotels or call for one. Taxis to Keflavík International Airport have fixed rates: ISK13,000 for 1–4 passengers or ISK16,000 for 5–8 passengers. **Taxi Reykjavík** offers 24-hour service.

Travelling by Ferry

Ferries run to a number of offshore islands. Daily services operated by **Eimskip** go to the Westman Islands from Landeyjahöfn in the south (about 30 mins). **Samskip** ferries run to Grímsey and Hrísey in the north, and Stykkishólmur–Flatey–Brjánslækur in the west.

Travelling by Bicycle

Cycling is an inexpensive way of seeing the country in summer, though come prepared for unsealed gravel roads and unkind weather. You need to be fit, experienced in repairing your bike, and to carry spares. You also need a tent and cooking gear and supplies, as there can be considerable distances between towns. There are several bike-hire shops in Reykjavík and Akureyri, but little assistance elsewhere. It is only permitted to cycle on roads or marked tracks.

Travelling on Foot

Iceland has many hiking trails. Accommodation is either camping or using hiking-organization huts. Both need to be pre-booked. Come equipped for bad weather and rough terrain (including river crossings). Carry all necessary gear, such as food, water and maps or a GPS. Some routes may also require crampons and an ice axe. Iceland's two hiking organizations, **Útivist** and **Ferðafélag Íslands**, can offer advice.

Travelling by Horse

Iceland's unique, stocky horses arrived with the Vikings. In addition to walk, trot, gallop and canter, they have a "fifth gear", the tölt. Stables like **Íshestar** and **Eldhestar** offer everything from hour-long to multi-week expeditions.

DIRECTORY

ARRIVING BY AIR

Air Iceland Connect
🌐 airicelandconnect.com

BSÍ
📞 580 5400
🌐 bsi.is

Eagle Air
🌐 eagleair.is

Flybus
📞 580 5400
🌐 re.is/flybus

Icelandair
🌐 icelandair.com

Keflavík International Airport
🌐 kefairport.is

Reykjavík International Airport
🌐 isavia.is

WOW Air
🌐 wowair.co.uk

ARRIVING BY SEA

Smyril Line
📞 298 354 900
🌐 smyrilline.com

TRAVELLING BY BUS

Reykjavík Excursions
📞 580 5400
🌐 re.is

SBA-Norðurleið
📞 550 0700
🌐 sba.is

Sterna Travel
📞 551 1166
🌐 sternatravel.com

Strætó
📞 540 2700
🌐 straeto.is

TREX
📞 587 6000
🌐 trex.is

TRAVELLING BY CAR

Iceland Car Rental
📞 415 2500
🌐 icelandcarrental.is

Road Conditions
🌐 road.is

TRAVELLING BY TAXI

Taxi Reykjavík
📞 561 0000

TRAVELLING BY FERRY

Samskip
📞 458 8000
🌐 landflutningar.is/saefari

Eimskip
📞 433 2254
🌐 seatours.is

TRAVELLING ON FOOT

Ferðafélag Íslands
🌐 fi.is/en

Útivist
🌐 utivist.is/english

TRAVELLING BY HORSE

Eldhestar
🌐 eldhestar.is

Íshestar
🌐 ishestar.is

Practical Information

Passports and Visas

Visitors from the UK, Ireland, Canada, the EU, the USA, Australia, New Zealand and countries that are signed up to the Schengen Agreement do not need **visas** for Iceland for a visit under 90 days. To enter the country, your passport must be valid for 3 months beyond the date of your intended stay.

A number of countries including the **UK**, **US**, and **Canada** have consulates in Reykjavík and are able to provide limited consular assitance to their nationals.

Customs and Immigration

Passengers over 18 may import 200 cigarettes or 250 g (8.8 oz) of tobacco products. Those over 20 may also bring a litre of spirits, a litre of wine and 6 litres of beer. Visitors can import 3 kg (7 lb) of food duty-free, but no meat unless canned or boiled. Riding clothing and angling gear must be disinfected and certified by a vet before entry. Used riding gear cannot be brought.

Vehicles, with up to 200 litres (44 gal) of fuel in built-in fuel tanks, can be brought in tax-free on the Smyril Line ferry to Seyðisfjörður, providing that you stay less than a year in Iceland, use the vehicle for personal travel only and take it with you on leaving. European drivers who bring their own vehicles do not need a Green Card or proof of third-party insurance; but, international automobile insurance may be required. Check with **Icelandic customs**.

Travel Safety Advice

Visitors can get up-to-date travel safety information from the **UK Foreign and Commonwealth Office**, the **US Department of State**, and the **Australian Department of Foreign Affairs and Trade**.

Travel Insurance

Taking out travel and health insurance is highly recommended and advisable. Check any policy exclusions, especially if planning on hiking or adventure travel. Also check whether you are already covered through your bank.

Health

No vaccinations are required for Iceland. You are advised to bring all medications you might need with you. All EU citizens holding an EHIC card are eligible for the same level of state health-care as they would receive at home, but other visitors have to pay. Iceland's major hospitals include **Akureyri Hospital** and **Landspítali University Hospital.** Ambulances incur a nonrefundable cost. Pharmacies *(apótek)* are in almost every town and often stay open until late. Prescription prices vary. Tap water is safe to drink everywhere in Iceland. Bring warm, wind- and waterproof clothes as the weather can be unpredictable. You'll also need sun-glasses, sunscreen and a hat, especially if you are planning to hike. Hikers also need tough boots for lava, snow and rain.

Be aware of natural hazards: you'll find very few warning signs or safety barriers even at heavily touristed sights such as waterfalls, geysers or boiling mud pits. Unbridged river crossings are dangerous, whether on foot or in a vehicle. Hiking trails are often poorly marked; hikers should be able to navigate in poor conditions. Avalanches have claimed many lives in Iceland over the years; you should always check warnings before hiking, especially in the West and East Fjords. If swimming, be aware that the coastline and beaches are typically not guarded.

Personal Security

Iceland is a safe country, with a low crime rate, but the usual advice applies. Always lock your car, don't leave valuables on display and don't flash your cash. Keep an extra eye on your belongings when you are in crowds, on public transport or queuing at busy tourist attractions. Minor assaults, petty burglary and drug-related crimes do occur, primarily in Reykjavík. Sexual harass-ment is not a common problem. However, in busy bars and clubs late at night women should take special care.

Penalties for possession, use and trafficking of drugs are severe, with large fines and custodial sentences. Iceland's police officers (lögreglan) carry pepper spray and extendable batons but, with the exception of airport police, no firearms.

Emergency Services

Various helplines are available to deal with any crisis. Call the emergency number if you need urgent **police** services, a **fire** brigade or an **ambulance**.

Travellers with Specific Needs

Iceland is fairly aware of the needs of travellers with secific needs, with urban hotels, restaurants, businesses and transport links either accessible or able to provide the relevant services if notified in advance. **Sjálfsbjörg Association for Disabled People** does not directly cater to tourists, but may provide advice.

Currency and Banking

Iceland's currency is the króna (ISK) or krónur in the plural. You can bring up to the equivalent of €10,000 into the country. Foreign currency is accepted at Keflavík International Airport and in a few shops in Reykjavík. Banks are found in all major towns, many with 24-hour ATMs outside issuing krónur. You'll also find ATMs in larger stores, malls and at petrol stations. MasterCard and Visa are widely accepted by ATMs

and businesses across the country but many places won't handle American Express, or accept cards to pay for purchases totalling less than ISK500. Check with your local bank before travelling to see if you can use your card abroad, and to find out the surcharges that will be levied to your account.

Telephone and Internet

Iceland's country code is 354; phone numbers within Iceland are seven digits long, with no area codes. All domestic calls are charged at a local rate, cheapest 7pm–8am Monday–Friday. Overseas calls are cheaper 7pm–8am every day for Europe and 11pm–8am every day for elsewhere. In the phonebook, people are listed in order of first name, not surname. The mobile phone network is reliable along the coast. It is a GSM system, compatible with European networks but not US ones. Buy a prepaid local SIM card if yours doesn't work here. Central Iceland has Nordic Mobile Telephone (NMT) coverage, but you should only need this if you're travelling independently in the Interior. Contact vehicle-rental companies or hiking organizations about renting an NMT set.

Iceland has one of the world's highest per capita internet usage rates. Free Wi-Fi is available in many cafés and in some accommodation. Tourist offices and libraries usually have computers available for public use.

DIRECTORY

PASSPORTS AND VISAS

Canada
MAP K2 ▪ Túngata 14, Reykjavík
w canada.is

UK
MAP L3 ▪ Laufásvegur 31, Reykjavík
w britishembassy.is

US
MAP L3 ▪ Laufásvegur 21, Reykjavík
w is.usembassy.gov

Visas
w utl.is

CUSTOMS AND IMMIGRATION

Icelandic Customs
w customs.is

TRAVEL SAFETY ADVICE

Australian Department of Foreign Affairs and Trade
w dfat.gov.au
w smartraveller.gov.au

UK Foreign and Commonwealth Office
w gov.uk/foreign-traveladvice

US Department of State
w state.gov/travel

HEALTH

Akureyri Hospital
Eyrarlandsvegur
[463 0100

Landspítali University Hospital
MAP M4 ▪ Hringbraut 101, Reykjavík
[543 1000

EMERGENCY SERVICES

Police, Fire and Ambulance
[112

TRAVELLERS WITH SPECIFIC NEEDS

Sjálfsbjörg Association for Disabled People
[550 0360
w sjalfsbjorg.is

Postal Services

Post offices are in most major towns and are open 9am–4:30pm Monday–Friday, sometimes closing later in larger towns. Check website for further details on **Reykjavík central post office**. Stamps are also sold in hotels, book-shops and supermarkets.

TV, Newspapers and Magazines

There are nine free TV channels in Iceland. Much of the content is in English and subtitled. Many hotels have satellite TV and screen major sporting events such as international and Premiership football.

Morgunblaðið, Fréttablaðið and *DV* are the main Icelandic newspapers. Both *Morgunblaðið* and *Fréttablaðið* have English summaries of the news on their websites. **Iceland Review** is a monthly English-speaking lifestyle magazine with a heavy tourist slant. Its website also offers a round-up of news stories. Free English-language newspaper **Grapevine** offers a lively view of the day's major issues, and is also a good what's-on guide for Reykjavík. English-language newspapers and magazines are available in hotels and bookshops, or for free in libraries.

Language

Icelandic is a difficult, complex language, with grammar similar in some ways to German or Latin, and few foreigners even attempt to learn it. English is taught in Iceland from an early age and most people speak it well, although Icelanders will be happy to hear you speak in their mother tongue.

Opening Hours

Office hours are 9am–5pm Monday–Friday, changing to 8am–4pm during the months of June, July and August. Shops are open 10am–6pm Monday–Friday, and Saturday from 10am until between 1pm and 4pm. Some supermarkets are open daily until 11pm. Banks are open 9:15am–4pm Monday–Friday. Outside Reykjavík, the hours may be shorter. Museums have their own opening hours, and outside the capital they might be closed in winter.

Businesses, banks and most shops are closed on the following holidays: New Year's Day, Maundy Thursday, Good Friday, Easter Sunday, Easter Monday, First Day of Summer (usually third Thursday in April), Labour Day (1 May), Ascension Day, Whit Sunday, Whit Monday, National Day (17 June), Bank Holiday (first Monday in August), Christmas Eve (from noon), Christmas Day, 26 December and New Year's Eve (from noon).

Time Difference

Iceland follows Greenwich Mean Time (GMT) and is 5 hours ahead of US Eastern Standard Time. It does not observe Daylight Saving Time.

Electrical Appliances

Iceland has standard European electrical voltage and frequency (240 V, 50 Hz) so North American electrical devices will need converters. Plugs are European-style two-pin. UK and North American electrical appliances will need a special adapter.

Driving

All European and US driving licences are valid in Iceland. UK visitors need to bring both parts of their licence. Visitors from other countries should check what they need with their local motoring organizations. Fuel is priced by the litre. Self-service pumps are cheaper than attended ones. Atlantsolía (AO) and ÓB are the cheapest brands. Fill up when you can as smaller towns might not have pumps and they can be far apart. Most filling stations are open until 11:30pm. Those in large towns and Reykjavík often have automatic payment available after closing time, which accepts notes and Visa credit cards. Some pumps in the countryside are completely automated.

Weather

Iceland's summer sun barely dips below the horizon at midnight. In winter you are lucky to get 4 hours of daylight, making November to February perfect for watching the aurora borealis. The climate is milder than you might expect. In the south of the country, winters average a bearable 0°C (32°F), while summer temperatures can reach 23°C (74°F), though rains can be frequent from spring to autumn. The north is generally colder, with heavy snowfalls in winter and temperatures dropping below -15°C (5°F), though the north-east is famously sunny in summer. The centre of the country is dominated by Vatnajökull, Europe's largest icecap, and the Highland Interior is unin-habited and usually snowbound for much of the year. Roads only open for a few weeks from mid-July until September.

Visitor Information

Good sources of general tourist information include the websites of the **Iceland Tourist Board**, **Promote Iceland**, **Randburg Travellers' Guide**, **Visit Reykjavík** and **Iceland Today**. For hikers and anglers, **Nordic Adventure Travel** is also useful. Forlagið and Ferðakort publish road atlases and specialist maps that cover the country in detail and are useful for independent touring and angling. You can buy a good range at book-shops in Reykjavík and Akureyri, plus a restricted selection at some tourist offices, supermarkets and roadhouses. Hiking organizations and the Icelandic National Parks office publish local maps, which are usually only available on site.

Trips and Tours

The **Golden Circle** tour run by Reykjavík Excursions is a classic combination of history and landscape, all with-in a stone's throw of Reykjavík. It takes in the Geysir hot springs, Gullfoss waterfalls and

Þingvellir National Park. Reykjavík Excursions also run tours to **Lakagígar**, one of the world's largest lava fields and site of the terrible 1783 eruption.

Askja, a hellish landscape of steaming volcanic craters in the northeast Interior, is where astronauts once trained for their moon landings and makes for an interesting day trip from Lake Mývatn.

For mountain trekking, try an introductory morning of ice climbing or a hardcore ascent of Hvannadalshnúkur (Iceland's highest peak) with specialist tour company **Icelandic Mountain Guides**.

Take a half-day **whale-watching** cruise from Húsavík in the north-east, or for **puffin watching**, catch a boat out to Lundey or Akurey near Reykjavík for a sight of these entertaining seabirds.

Swimming

Bring your swimming gear as every town has a public pool (sundlaug), geothermally heated to a constant temperature of 28°C (83°F) and often with attached hot tubs and sau-nas. They are inexpensive, and many spend hours at them every day. There is a strict pool etiquette to be followed: make sure you take your shoes off before entering the changing rooms, and shower with-out your costume before entering the pool area.

Out in the wilds, there are also many natural geothermal springs in places such as Mývatn, Landmannalaugar, and the artificial Blue Lagoon,

which offer a fantastically atmospheric experience, especially during the winter months.

Shopping

Imported goods will be more expensive than they would be at home, but a number of local products make good-value souvenirs. Icelandic woollen jumpers are available from shops but, as many are home-made sizes and proportions can be random and you'll have to try on several until you find a good fit.

Smoked salmon, trout and Arctic char are excellent and cheapest if bought at supermarkets or directly from smokehouses. You'll need to check that you're allowed to import them into your home country.

Outdoor clothing by 66°N and Cintamani is stylishly designed and of high quality, though not cheap. Silver and lava jewellery is also popular. Note that anything made from sealskin cannot be imported into the US, though there are no such restrictions in the UK and Europe.

While there are no regular sale periods, shops tend to reduce prices in midsummer and in January. There are duty-free shops at Keflavík International Airport, where you can buy alcohol at reduced rates.

All prices include VAT, which on most goods is 25.5%. Tourists get a 15% **tax refund** on single items costing ISK6,000 or more. To get the refund, the shop will have to fill out a form for you when you are buying, then you can take the form and receipt to a refund booth at Keflavík airport, the Reykjavík tourist office Seyðisfjörður ferries, or any Reykjavík shopping mall.

Smoking

Smoking is prohibited in bars, restaurants, clubs and cafés. There are no designated smoking areas inside and smoking outside is also restricted to certain areas. It is forbidden to smoke on public transport.

Dining

There is some excellent local food, worth perhaps splashing out for once in a smart restaurant. Seafood is top of the list, with superb Atlantic salmon, cod, trout, and char, not to mention lobster. Icelandic lamb is also very good. At certain times of the year you can find oddities such as smoked puffin, traditionally harvested in southern Iceland, though populations are plummeting and there has been an embargo on catching these birds. Other traditional foods include *harðfiskur* (wind-dried cod), a popular snack sometimes eaten with butter; *hangikjöt* (smoked lamb); *rjúpa* (ptarmigan), a grouse-like game bird; *súrmatur* (meats pickled in whey); and *hákarl* (fermented shark), an eye-wateringly pungent speciality.

There are smart but expensive restaurants in Reykjavík, Akureyri and other large towns. You can keep costs down by sticking to the specials board or a fixed menu if available. There are less pricey Thai, Indian, Italian and Chinese places, where you can eat without bankrupting yourself, but the food is not particularly memorable. Many places offer kids portions. It is not customary to leave a tip however a service charge will be included in the final bill.

There are cafés all over the country – Reykjavík even has its own chain, Kaffitár. They often allow at least one free refill. Aside from cafés, the cheapest places to eat out are roadhouse restaurants, which are sometimes the only places serving cooked food in an area. Their menus are filling rather than exciting – pizza, burgers, chips and *pylsur* (hot dogs) – but there's usually an inexpensive set menu featuring soup and bread, often with a free refill. Museums and cultural centres often have bargain-priced eateries serving lunch and coffee – no entry fee required to dine here.

In terms of self-catering, Bónus, Krónan, Samkaup and Kjarval are the most widespread supermarkets, with Bónus charging the lowest prices. Most villages will have somewhere to stock up, but the range might be limited and opening hours are often short in the countryside. In winter, supermarkets sometimes provide free coffee for shoppers. In summer, fresh vegetables are easily available, especially in hothouse towns, where they are grown using geothermal methods. Many villages have bakeries, but rarely butchers or fishmongers. More information on Icelandic dining can be found on the **Iceland Local Food Guide**.

Drinking

Alcohol is sold through state-controlled shops (Vínbúðin) and is highly taxed; you'll save money by bringing in your full duty-free allowance. Vínbúðin have very restricted, totally unpredictable opening hours, and outside Reykjavík tend to be tucked away in obscure corners. The local spirit of choice is *brennivín* – basically, vodka flavoured with caraway and angelica. Iceland imports all of its wine, with the exception of one brand, Kvöldsól, which is made in Húsavík from blueberries, crowberries and rhubarb. The cheapest beer are the locally brewed Viking Gold and Thule. Because of the cost of alcohol, it is considered normal not to buy rounds, and even to sip on one drink for the entire evening, though many bars have happy hours. Locals often drink at home before going out for the night.

Accommodation

Iceland's increasing popularity has put a pressure on summer accommodation. It is advised to book beds in advance – even for hostels. Online booking is the norm everywhere.

It is suggested that you should always camp at a campsite. Check the **Environment Agency of Iceland** for more details on camping and campsites. Most people opt to use the well-equipped and inexpensive campsites found in even the smallest village. Most have toilets and showers. If there are no showers, head to the nearest public swimming pool. Make sure you have a weatherproof tent, a groundsheet, guy ropes and a variety of pegs, as rough ground and gale-force winds are a fact of life. The discount **Camping Card** will help campers save money across multiple campsites throughout the country.

In popular hiking areas, you will also find mountain huts run by the hiking organizations. These are usually chalet-style buildings, with dormitories, kitchens, toilets, showers and bunks or mattresses. Beds must be booked in advance and bring a sleeping bag.

There are 33 official **hostels**, ranging from a turf-roofed hut to multi-storey affairs with TVs, kitchens, cafés and tour desks. Hostel members get a discount on the room rate. Dormitories are the norm, but some have private rooms. Bring a sleeping bag or hire bedsheets if available.

Part-way between hostels and hotels, urban guesthouses and rural farmstays offer a broad range of self-catering facilities, sometimes in a main building, sometimes in separate chalets. For more information on farm holidays, visit **Hey Iceland**. Doubles or family rooms with made-up beds are usual, though some places offer a cheaper-rate option of sleeping bag accommodation, where you supply your own bedding. For an extra charge, meals can be arranged in advance.

Every town in Iceland has a hotel of some sort. Many formal hotels open year-round and tend to be stuffy affairs, run by the airlines or a local company. Privately run businesses tend to have far more character. They are usually warm, well-equipped places with restaurants, bars and sometimes conference facilities, but peak summer rates are very expensive for what you get. International airlines can offer attractive flight-and-accommodation packages and you'll find that prices drop considerably outside the main summer tourist season. An alternative is to use one of the 12 summer-only **Hotel Eddas** scattered around the country, which serve as schools for the rest of the year. Rates are lower than ordinary hotels and although rooms are functional, facilities are not too bad, often with restaurants or cafés, swimming pools and even local tours available.

DIRECTORY

SHOPPING

Tax Refund
w tollur.is

DINING

Iceland Local Food Guide
w icelandlocalfood.is

ACCOMMODATION

The Environment Agency of Iceland
w ust.is/einstaklingar

Camping Card
w campingcard.is

Hey Iceland
w www.heyiceland.is

Hostels
w hostel.is

Hotel Eddas
w hoteledda.is

Places to Stay

PRICE CATEGORIES
For a standard double room per night (with breakfast if included), including taxes and extra charges.

ⓚ under ISK20,000   ⓚⓚ ISK20,000–40,000
ⓚⓚⓚ over ISK40,000

Hotels in the Centre of Reykjavík

Fosshotel Lind
MAP N3 ■ Rauðarárstígur 18 ■ 562 3350 ■ www.fosshotel.is ■ ⓚⓚ
A reliable, comfortable hotel with good facilities and helpful staff. There is nothing lacking in the services offered, but the rooms are on the small and simple side. However, it is good for a brief stay.

Hlemmur Square
MAP B5 ■ Laugarvegur 105 ■ 415 1600 ■ www.hlemmursquare.com ■ ⓚⓚ
This boutique hotel offers 17 spacious single and double rooms. Most rooms have balconies with scenic views of the city's colourful rooftops. The bar has an extensive choice of Icelandic craft beers on tap and the restaurant offers bistro-style menu. Hostel facilities are also available on the premises.

Hótel Klöpp
MAP M2 ■ Klapparstígur 26 ■ 595 8520 ■ www.centerhotels.com ■ ⓚⓚ
This is a streamlined place with comfortable rooms and open-plan bathrooms. Friendly, efficient and located just off bustling Laugarvegur, it is a sound option for a short stay. Rooms on the upper floors are quieter and some have sea views.

Hótel Óðinsvé
MAP L3 ■ Þórsgata 1 ■ 511 6200 ■ www.hotelodinsve.is ■ ⓚⓚ
Excellent value hotel that manages to balance the homey 1930s building with modern minimalist chic. Its location off the main streets means less likelihood of being disturbed by rowdy weekend merrymakers. The bistro-style SNAPS restaurant specializes in grills.

Hótel Borg
MAP L2 ■ Pósthússtræti 11 ■ 551 1440 ■ www.hotelborg.is ■ ⓚⓚⓚ
Wonderful Art Deco building where old time elegance and modern style is reflected in the immaculate rooms, which are a showcase in sophistication, complete with genuine period furnishings and luxurious facilities such as heated bathroom marble floors.

Hótel Holt
MAP L3 ■ Bergstaðastræti 37 ■ 552 5700 ■ www.hotelholt.is ■ ⓚⓚⓚ
Holt's unappealing façade is deceptive – once through the doors you are in one of the most plush old-style hotels in town. It has the country's largest privately owned collection of 19th-century Icelandic artworks and an outstanding restaurant.

Hótel Plaza
MAP K2 ■ Aðalstræti 4–6 ■ 595 8550 ■ www.centerhotels.com ■ ⓚⓚ
Light, airy, modern building with rooms to match – timber flooring, white walls and furnishings. The suites have views of the older part of the city and there is an excellent choice of good restaurants nearby.

Hótel Reykjavík Centrum
MAP K2 ■ Aðalstræti 16 ■ 514 6000 ■ www.hotelcentrum.is ■ ⓚⓚⓚ
A modern hotel in an old building: the timber and red-corrugated-iron exterior sits above the remains of a 7th-century Viking settlement. The rooms have been tastefully modernized and there is a renowned restaurant on the premises.

Reykjavík 101
MAP L2 ■ Hverfisgata 10 ■ 580 0101 ■ www.101hotel.is ■ ⓚⓚⓚ
Close to the capital's main shopping street, this smart hotel is stark on the outside. Inside, the modern, bright rooms have a contemporary minimalist look, complete with wooden flooring, large beds and marble bathrooms. Amenities include a gym and spa.

Hotels Around Reykjavík

Hótel Cabin
MAP N3 ■ Borgartún 32, 105 Reykjavík ■ 511 6030 ■ www.hotelcabin.is ■ ⓚ
Tidy budget hotel with basic but clean

furnishings and compact rooms. Upper floors have ocean views, while some rooms are designed with inward-facing windows for relief during the bright summer nights. Great-value lunch buffet at the restaurant.

Hótel Laxnes
MAP Q5 ▪ Háholt 7, 270 Mosfellsbær ▪ 566 8822 ▪ www.hotellaxnes.is ▪ Ⓚ
A hotel in a semi-rural location, about a 20-minute bus ride from Reykjavík. The double rooms and apartments with kitchenettes are especially good and there's an outdoor hot tub with mountain views. There is a golf course and swimming pool nearby, and regular shuttle buses into town.

Reykjavík City Hostel
MAP R3 ▪ Sundlaugarvegur 34, 105 Reykjavík ▪ 553 8110 ▪ www.hostel.is ▪ Ⓚ
One of the few Icelandic HI Hostels with private rooms as well as dormitories, which, along with its location near the Botanic Gardens and Laugardalur swimming pool, makes it the best budget option in town. Booking in advance is recommended.

Viking Village
MAP P6 ▪ Strandgata 55, 220 Hafnarfjörður ▪ 565 1213 ▪ www.fjorukrain.is ▪ Ⓚ
A whole complex built around a Viking theme, with accommodation, restaurants and Viking entertainment. The exterior of the hotel has a slight warehouse feel, but the rooms are surprisingly good. There are also 14 Viking-themed cottages near the hotel.

22 Hill Hotel
MAP N3 ▪ Brautarholt 22–24, 105 Reykjavík ▪ 511 3777 ▪ www.22hillhotel.is ▪ ⓀⓀ
Despite the drab exterior, the decent-sized rooms with friendly staff, excellent views, prime location, and good restaurant make this mid-priced option a firm favourite among visitors to the capital.

Hótel Ísland
MAP R4 ▪ Ármúli 9, 108 Reykjavík ▪ 595 7000 ▪ www.hotelisland.is ▪ ⓀⓀ
Centrally located next to the city's financial district and Laugardalur valley, Hótel Ísland is Iceland's first dedicated wellness and medical hotel. It features 129 comfortable rooms, with many offering views of the mountains surrounding Reykjavík. There's also a spa and a bistro serving modern international cuisine.

Hótel Örkin
MAP P4 ▪ Brautarholt 29, 105 Reykjavík ▪ 568 0777 ▪ www.hotelorkin.is ▪ ⓀⓀ
Small budget hotel run by the Faroese Seamen's Mission, Örkin has a friendly atmosphere. The room prices include breakfast and freshly baked cakes in the afternoon.

Blue Lagoon Retreat
MAP B5 ▪ Norðurljosavegur 11, 240 Grindavík ▪ 420 8700 ▪ www.bluelagoon.com ▪ ⓀⓀⓀⓀ
A modern haven situated in the heart of nature, Blue Lagoon Retreat offers 62 luxurious suites, and private thermal spa areas. Floor-to-ceiling windows overlook the surrounding volcanic landscape. The restaurant has a tasting menu.

Grand Hótel Reykjavík
MAP Q3 ▪ Sigtún 38, 105 Reykjavík ▪ 514 8000 ▪ www.grand.is ▪ ⓀⓀⓀ
Iceland's second largest hotel is situated in an impressive tower block. It has a modern restaurant and a cosy and attractive fitness centre and spa. The conference rooms make it an ideal business venue.

Hilton Reykjavík Nordica
MAP Q4 ▪ Suðurlandsbraut 2, 108 Reykjavík ▪ 444 5000 ▪ www.hiltonreykjavik.com ▪ ⓀⓀⓀ
As the name suggests, the decor here is distinctly biased towards monochromatic furnishings and pine flooring. The in-room safes and blackout curtains (for the luminous summer nights) are a nice touch.

Radisson Blu Saga Hótel
MAP J3 ▪ Hagatorg, 107 Reykjavík ▪ 525 9900 ▪ www.radissonblu.com ▪ ⓀⓀⓀ
Located close to the city centre, this business and conference venue enjoys lovely views. The master suite is very stylish, with dark wooden floors and a private balcony. All guests have access to the beauty centre and gym.

Hotels Around Iceland

Hótel Búðir

MAP A4 ■ 356 Snæfellsnes ■ 435 6700 ■ www.budir.is ■ ⓀⓀ
This elegantly refurbished old-style hotel is one of Iceland's romantic gems. It has an atmospheric seaside setting, with only a dark wooden church and the nearby white cone of Snæfellsjökull for company. The restaurant is renowned for it's fresh fish and lamb dishes.

Hótel Framtíð

MAP G4 ■ Vogaland 4, 765 Djúpivogur ■ 478 8887 ■ www.hotel framtid.com ■ ⓀⓀ
This delightful old building overlooks the attractive village harbour of Djúpivogur and is a good place to rest after a trip to Papey island. There are modern rooms in the main hotel and ordinary wooden cabins for hire, as well as a nearby campsite.

Hótel Gígur

MAP F2 ■ Skútustaðir, 600 Mývatn ■ 464 4455 ■ www.keahotels.is ■ ⓀⓀ
This well managed, modern hotel on the southern shore of Mývatn has amazing views out over the lake from the dining room. Watch out for the flies outside the lobby during the summer. Free Wi-Fi in every room.

Hótel Ísafjörður

MAP B2 ■ Silfurtorg 2, 400 Ísafjörður ■ 456 4111 ■ www.hotelisafjordur.is ■ ⓀⓀ
The solid exterior, providing protection against the severe winter storms, hides a warm, comfortable

and friendly hotel. The staff go out of their way to be helpful. The rooms are not huge, but have everything you will need for a night or two. The restaurant is decent, if slightly on the expensive side.

Hótel KEA

MAP E2 ■ Hafnarstræti 87–89, 600 Akureyri ■ 460 2000 ■ www.kea hotels.is ■ ⓀⓀ
Located in the heart of Akureyri, this is the flagship hotel in North Iceland of the KEA chain. The rooms are well furnished and quite spacious. There is a bistro and bar, and the generous buffet breakfast is the ideal start to the day.

Hotel Skaftafell

MAP F5 ■ Freysnes, 785 Öræfi ■ 478 1945 ■ www. hotelskaftafell.is ■ ⓀⓀ
This hotel is a perfectly comfortable base for hiking at nearby Skaftafell National Park. Most of the 63 rooms afford breathtaking glacier views.

Icelandair Hótel Hamar

MAP B4 ■ Golfvöllurinn Hamar, 310 Borgarnes ■ 433 6600 ■ www.ice landairhotels.com ■ ⓀⓀ
This long, low hotel in a peaceful setting comes complete with outdoor hot tubs, a top-notch restaurant and an excellent 18-hole golf course. There are great mountain views and each room has a large window and a door opening directly onto the grounds. Do not miss out on a visit to the Borgarnes Settlement Centre during your stay here.

Icelandair Hótel Hérað

MAP G3 ■ Miðvangur 5-7, 700 Egilsstaðir ■ 471 1500 ■ www.icelandair hotels.com ■ ⓀⓀ
The bleak, grey exterior of this hotel should not deter you from staying here. Inside, the large rooms are tastefully furnished and another bonus is the helpful staff. Along with the on-site restaurant try Café Nielsen (see p105), located up the road in the oldest house in town and open in summer only.

Icelandair Hótel Klaustur

MAP E5 ■ Klausturvegur 6, 880 Kirkjubæjarklaustur ■ 487 4900 ■ www.iceland airhotels.com ■ ⓀⓀ
It may seem strange to find such a large hotel in such a tiny place, but Icelandair Hótel Klaustur is well placed for summer excursions to Skaftafell National Park and the Lakagígar craters. Besides its great location, this hotel also offers a decent restaurant and a bar with an outdoor terrace on site, as well as a small heated pool next door.

Leirubakki

MAP D5 ■ Leirubakki ■ 487 8700 ■ www. leirubakki.is ■ ⓀⓀ
What makes this comfortable, simple modern hotel exceptional is its location in the heart of south Iceland and within sight of the smouldering ridge of Hekla, one of Iceland's most active volcanoes. Guests can enjoy the outdoor natural thermal spring built of lava blocks with beautiful views.

Hótel Rangá
MAP C5 ▪ Ringroad, near Hella ▪ 487 5700 ▪ www.hotelranga.is ▪ Ⓚ Ⓚ Ⓚ
This countryside retreat, with 4-star comforts, is especially convenient if salmon fishing on the nearby Rangá river. The lodge-style pine cabins and main buildings are perfectly decorated and there is an excellent restaurant. As well as the river, it is also close to all of south Iceland's best attractions.

Guesthouses

Gistiheimilið Baldursbrá
MAP L4 ▪ Laufásvegur 41, 101 Reykjavík ▪ 552 6646 ▪ Ⓚ
Located in a residential area, this family-run place provides spacious rooms with shared bathrooms and an outdoor hot tub for a very reasonable price.

Gistiheimilið Hamar
MAP C6 ▪ Herjolfsgata 4, Heimaey, Vestmannaeyjar ▪ 481 3400 ▪ Open May–Sep ▪ www.guesthousehamar.is ▪ Ⓚ
This modern block near the harbour has large rooms that sleep up to four guests, with private bathrooms. Breakfast is available for patrons.

Gistiheimilið Sunna
MAP M3 ▪ Þórsgata 26, 101 Reykjavík ▪ 511 5570 ▪ www.sunna.is ▪ Ⓚ
Close to Hallgrímskirkja, this guesthouse offers clean rooms with access to a kitchenette, and shared or private bathrooms. A buffet breakfast is included. Noise can be a problem in the late-partying city.

Kex Hostel
MAP B5 ▪ Skúlagata 28, 101 Reykjavík ▪ 561 6060 ▪ www.kexhostel.is ▪ Ⓚ
Vibrant and colourful, Kex Hostel is housed inside a renovated biscuit factory. It has comfortable dorms for up to 16 people as well as private rooms. The decor is welcoming with vintage furniture dotted around the spacious lobby and an on-site gastropub.

Lava Hostel
MAP B5 ▪ Hjallabraut 51, 220 Hafnarfjörður ▪ 565 0900 ▪ www.lavahostel.is ▪ Ⓚ
This simple, self-catering guesthouse has two to eight beds per room, shared bathrooms and full kitchen facilities. There is also a dormitory with sleeping-bag accommodation (bring your own or rent linen here). Buses to Reykjavík, and the international airport, stop nearby.

Skálholtsskóli
MAP C5 ▪ Skalholt ▪ 486 8870 ▪ www.skalholt.is ▪ Ⓚ
The guesthouse is attached to the Skálholt Center – a historic cultural venue run by the Evangelical Lutheran Church of Iceland. Summer concerts at the cathedral are a bonus Besides double and single rooms, Skálholtsskóli also offers sleeping bag services. Book in advance.

Sólheimar Eco-Village
MAP C5 ▪ Grímsnes, 801 Selfoss ▪ 480 4483 ▪ www.solheimar.is ▪ Ⓚ
A stay in this world renowned sustainable community, founded in 1930, is an unforgettable experience. As well as the comfortable guesthouse with access to a swimming pool and hot tub, there are crafts workshops, a café and a sculpture garden.

Gistiheimilið Hof
MAP A4 ▪ Hofgarðar, 365 Snæfellsbær ▪ 846 3897 ▪ www.gistihof.is ▪ Ⓚ Ⓚ
Long, turf-roofed building in a panoramic rural location near to a sandy beach. The guesthouse has six self-contained units, with three double bedrooms, a bathroom, kitchenette and outdoor hot tub. There are 16 en-suite rooms available in the summer.

Gistihúsið Egilsstöðum
MAP G3 ▪ Egilsstaðir ▪ 471 1114 ▪ www.lakehotel.is ▪ Ⓚ Ⓚ
With a cosy family-run atmosphere this comfortable hotel is set in a large renovated farmhouse just outside of town and with great views over the lake. Rooms are all en-suite. There is a great restaurant, Eldhúsið, on the first floor and a spa, Baðhúsið, on the ground floor.

Litli Geysir Hotel
MAP C5 ▪ Haukadalur 35, 801 Selfoss ▪ 486 8733 ▪ www.geysircenter.is ▪ Ⓚ Ⓚ
Located just opposite the geothermal springs, Litli Geysir is a great choice for group accommodation. The hotel offers 22 rooms with the breakfast included in the price. They have a telescope in the lounge and the adjoining Geysir Centre has a café and two restaurants.

For a key to hotel price categories see p128

Puffin Hotel Vík

MAP D6 ▪ Vikurbraut 26, Vík ▪ 467 1212 ▪ www. puffinhotelvik.is ▪ ⓚⓚ

Both a charming hotel and hostel, Puffin has 22 en-suite rooms set between a modern building, dating from 2011, and an older wing. A separate hostel building offers 11 cheaper rooms in various sizes with cooking facilities and shared bathrooms. You can also choose to stay in one of the apartments.

Summer Hotels and Eddas

Hólar í Hjaltadal

MAP D2 ▪ Hólar, near Sauðárkrókur ▪ 849 6348 ▪ Open Jun–Aug ▪ www. holar.is/en ▪ ⓚ

The small community of Hólar is home to a historically important cathedral, the island's largest estate and Hólar University, where student accommodation is available to tourists.

Hótel Edda Höfn

MAP G5 ▪ Höfn ▪ 444 4850 ▪ Open May–Sep ▪ www.hoteledda.is ▪ ⓚ

Well placed for glacier trips to Vatnajökull or hiking in the Lónsöræfi reserve, these school buildings offer straight-forward double rooms and dorms with shared bathrooms and toilets, plus a restaurant that serves breakfast.

Hótel Edda Skógar

MAP D6 ▪ Skógar ▪ 444 4830 ▪ Open Jun–Aug ▪ www.hoteledda.is ▪ ⓚ

Storm-proof building neighbouring one of Iceland's most impressive waterfalls, Skogafoss,

the eccentric Skógar Museum and the superb hiking trail to Þórsmörk. Plain, serviceable rooms with shared bathroom facilities, sleeping-bag space and a restaurant serving a plentiful breakfast buffet and à la carte dinner are available.

Hótel Edda Stórutjarnir

MAP E2 ▪ Stórutjarnir, Route 1 ▪ 444 4890 ▪ Open Jun–Aug ▪ www.hoteledda.is ▪ ⓚ

Conveniently located between Akureyri and Mývatn, this lakeside hotel sits in a short, tight valley frequented by geese in the summer. Rooms include private en-suite doubles as well as dormitories. There is also a restaurant and an outdoor swimming pool with a hot tub.

Hótel Hallormstaður

MAP G3 ▪ Hallormsstaður, near Egilsstaðir ▪ 471 2400 ▪ www.701hotels.is ▪ ⓚ

Cosy country hotel inside Iceland's most extensive forest, close to Lögurinn lake. The hotel has self-contained wooden cottages, rooms in a large guesthouse and summer-only accommodation. Guests can choose from two hotel restaurants.

Fosshótel Vatnajökull

MAP G5 ▪ Route 1 near Höfn, Hornafjörður ▪ 478 2555 ▪ www.fosshotel.is ▪ ⓚⓚ

This is a functional, tidy place, with warm but small and simply furnished rooms. Given the fantastic location,

you should get a room with glacier views which doesn't cost extra.

Hótel Aldan

MAP H3 ▪ Norðurgata 2, 710 Seyðisfjörður ▪ 472 1277 ▪ www.hotelaldan. is ▪ ⓚⓚ

A 19th-century wooden building by the harbour, once a bank, has been converted into this nine-bedroom hotel, which retains a historic atmosphere with period furnishings. There is a bar and an excellent restaurant. More rooms are available in the nearby sister operation, Hótel Snæfell, which is run by the same family.

Hótel Edda Ísafjörður

MAP B2 ▪ Torfnes, Ísafjörður ▪ 444 4960 ▪ Open Jun–Aug ▪ www. hoteledda.is ▪ ⓚⓚ

Located near the centre of Ísafjörður, this school (for most of the year) has good facilities. Rooms have en-suite bathrooms or in-room washbasins. There is a campsite and sleeping-bag space in the heated sports hall. Buffet breakfast is available.

Hótel Edda ML Laugarvatn

MAP C5 ▪ Laugarvatn ▪ 444 4810 ▪ Open Jun–Aug ▪ www.hoteledda.is ▪ ⓚⓚ

One of two Eddas in town, this huge complex offers double rooms that are either en-suite or have shared bathrooms. There is an in-house restaurant and it is close to the Golden Circle attractions, a huge pool and Laugarvatn lake.

Hótel Flókalundur
MAP C5 ■ Vatnsfirði, 451 Patreksfjörður ■ 456 2011 ■ Open May–Sep ■ www. flokalundur.is ■ ⓚⓚ
A family-run hotel, Flókalundur is located on the south coast of the Westfjords, within striking distance of Látrabjarg, Rauðasandur and Ísafjörður. The hotel has 15 comfortable rooms with spectacular views of the surrounding landscape.

Campsites and Character Stays

Egilsstaðir Campsite
MAP G3 ■ Kaupvangur 17, 700 Egilsstaðir ■ 470 0750 ■ www.visitegliss tadir.is ■ ⓚ
Scruffy and occasionally boggy camping ground with some sheltered woody patches near Egilsstaðir's tourist information and long-distance bus stop; you need to choose your site carefully. Good shower and toilet facilities and a tiny, sheltered bar becue and seating area.

Galtalækur II
MAP C5 ■ Route 26, Rangárþing ytra, Hella ■ 487 6528 ■ www.1.is/ gl2/en ■ ⓚ
Galtalækur II offers a pleasant campsite and self-contained cabins near Þangavatn lake, Þjótatoss waterfall and Hekla volcano. You can buy fishing licences here.

Hamrar Campsite
MAP E2 ■ Kjarnaskógur, Akureyri ■ 461 2264 ■ www.hamrar.is ■ ⓚ
Enormous camping grounds near woodland outside Akureyri in the north of the island. You do not need to reserve a space in advance. There are toilets, hot showers, washing machines and tumble dryers on site, along with a kitchen and a covered dining area.

Hlíð Campsite
MAP F2 ■ Reykjahlíð, Mývatn ■ 464 4103 ■ www.myvatnaccom modation.is ■ ⓚ
This is a great place to base yourself while at Mývatn; there are superb views over Reykjahlíð and the lake. The site offers hot showers, toilets and outdoor sinks for washing laundry or plates and cutlery. Wooden cabins and a dorm building are also available.

Hótel Dyrhólaey
MAP D6 ■ Near Vik ■ 487 1333 ■ www.dyrholaey.is ■ ⓚ
This lakeside farmstead is nestled in the hills above Dyrhólaey bird reserve. The fully equipped rooms come complete with private bathrooms and are clean, warm and very comfortable. North facing rooms have good views of the Mýrdalsjökull icecap. Staff are helpful and the restaurant offers a healthy breakfast and good-value evening buffet of Icelandic dishes.

Reykjavík Campsite
MAP R2 ■ Sundlaugar- vegur 32, 105 Reykjavík ■ 568 6944 ■ www.reyk javikcampsite.is ■ ⓚ
The huge grassy slope of this campsite has room for hundreds of tents. A 20-minute walk from the city centre, the site has a covered cooking area, washing machine, tumble dryer, toilets and showers.

Hótel Anna
MAP D6 ■ Moldnúpur, Route 246, between Skógar and Seljarlandsfoss ■ 487 8950 ■ www.hotel anna.is ■ ⓚⓚⓚ
Red-roofed farmhouse in a great rural location with Eyjafjallajökull rising above it. Large beds, low ceilings and old wooden furniture add to the character. Price includes breakfast and use of hot tubs and sauna.

Hótel Laki
MAP E5 ■ Efri Vík, Kirkjubæjarklaustur ■ 412 4600 ■ www. hotellaki.is ■ ⓚⓚⓚ
A converted farmhouse, the rooms at this hotel are all en-suite doubles. Located on the edge of a pseudocrater and a lava field stretching to Lakagígar, Hótel Laki is the perfect base for hikers and nature lovers.

Hótel Látrabjarg
MAP A2 ■ Near Route 612/615 junction, Patreksfjörður ■ 456 1500 ■ Open mid-May– Sep ■ www.latrabjarg. com ■ ⓚⓚⓚ
Originally a boarding school, this hotel is close to the beach and bird cliffs. Rooms have en-suite or shared bathrooms. Freshwater trout fishing is possible in the nearby Sauðlauksdalur lake for a small fee.

Hótel Tindastól
MAP D2 ■ Lindargata 3, Sauðárkrókur ■ 453 5002 ■ www.arctichotels.is ■ ⓚⓚⓚ
Iceland's oldest hotel opened in 1884 and has an outdoor spa. Rooms have a warm and cosy feel. A resident ghost adds to the atmosphere.

For a key to hotel price categories see p128

General Index

Acknowledgments

Author
David Leffman is a travel writer and photographer who first visited Iceland in 1981. He has authored *Eyewitness China* for DK, along with guidebooks to Iceland, Australia, Indonesia, China and Hong Kong for Rough Guides. He has also led specialist guided tours to China.

Contents Outline
Michael Kissane

Publishing Director Georgina Dee

Publisher Vivien Antwi

Design Director Phil Ormerod

Editorial Emma Brady, Michelle Crane, Rachel Fox, Freddie Marriage, Fíodhna Ní Ghríofa, Sally Schafer, Neil Simpson, Christine Stroyan

Cover Design Maxine Pedliham, Vinita Venugopal

Design Sunita Gahir

Picture Research Phoebe Lowndes, Susie Peachey, Ellen Root, Oran Tarjan

Cartography Stuart James, Zafar-ul-Islam Khan, Suresh Kumar, Casper Morris

DTP Jason Little, George Nimmo

Production Nancy-Jane Maun

Factchecker Paul Sullivan

Proofreader Kate Berens

Indexer Helen Peters

Phrase Book Bergljót Njóla Jakobsdóttir

Revisions Rebecca Flynn, Bharti Karakoti, Nayan Keshan, Sumita Khatwani, Shikha Kulkarni, Anuroop Sanwalia, Azeem Siddiqui, Rituraj Singh, Paul Sullivan, Vaishali Vashisht

Commissioned Photography Nigel Hicks, Rough Guides/David Leffman

Picture Credits
The publisher would like to thank the following for their kind permission to reproduce their photographs:
Key: a-above; b-below/bottom; c-centre; f-far; l-left; r-right; t-top

4Corners: SIME/Olimpio Fantuz 3tl, 72–3; SIM /Maurizio Rellini 56–7.

Alamy Images: Arctic Images 68bc; Icelandic photo agency 61br;Mary Evans Picture Library 36tl; Graham Prentice 74tl; Steven Sheppardson 37t.

Alamy Stock Photo: COMPAGNON Bruno 33br; PHOTOFVG RM COLLECTION 66crb.

Ásgeir Helgi & Agust G. Atlason: 68b.

Austur Club: Thorgeir Olafsson 60cla.

Corbis: Arctic-Images/SuperStock 70t; Arctic-Images 4b, 59tr, 52br, 116b; Hans Strand 115t.

Dreamstime.com: Sylvia Adams 32clb; Adreslebedev 4clb; Aiisha 4t; Steve Allen 22–3; Andreanita 24bl; Claudio Balducelli 20–21c; Gisli Baldursson 33tl, 51tr; Darius Baužys 13tl; Andrey Bayda 49tl; Bilderschorsch 104bl; Sigurdur William Brynjarsson 2tr, 34–5; Tomáš Bureš 47bc; Cadifor 103bc; Checco 50br, 54t; Chrishowey 71br; Demerzel21 2tl, 8–9, 105–106; Derwuth 76b; Filip Fuxa 7cr, 10bl, 46crb, 85bl; Gkoultouridis 16–7c; H368k742 59clb, 67tr; Jon Helgason 46tc; Humgate 7tr; Iaceo 6cl; Martín Zalba Ibanez 32br, 66t; Dmitry Islentyev 14bl; Jarcosa98crb; Javarman 30–31c; Jeremyreds 3tr, 118–19; Aagje De Jong 55cl; Þórarinn Jónsson 45b; Thomas Langlands 27tl; Florence Mcginn 28–9c, minnystock 11t; Erzsi Molnár 51cl; Oriontrail 77cla; Parys 48bl; Pedja77 50clb; Johann Ragnarsson 49crb; Michael Ransburg 18–19c, 71tl; Arseniy Rogov 48tc; Sanspek 4cla; Selitbul 52br; Serinus 4cl; Rafn Sigurbjörnsson 11crb; Marteinn Sigurdsson 90cra; Leonid Spektor 103cla; Kippy Spilker 13cb; Alexey Stiop 29cl; Takepicsforfun 4crb; Tatonka 96b; Ryan Taylor 10–11b; Milan_tesar 31bl; Alexey Tkachenko 60bc; Tomas1111 26cl, 39tl; Topdeq 24cl; Ucheema 4cra; Ukrphoto 63tr; Victorianl 11cra; Corepics Vof 30bl; Dennis Van De Water 14-5c; Wkruck 11c; Zbindere 89br.

Einar Jonsson Sculpture Museum: 40crb.

Fishmarkadurinn: Bjorn Arnason 63cl.

FLPA: Bill Coster 20b; ImageBroker 67br.

Getty Images: Bloomberg 37br; Patrick Dieudonne 86tc; Michele Falzone 42tr; Atli Mar Hafsteinsson 86bl; Thorsten Henn 53cl; Lonely Planet Images 6tr; Richard Manin 42bl; Martin Moos 88tl.

Grái Kötturinn: 80bl.

Icelandic Fish & Chips: 64b.

Inside the Volcano: Sølve Fredheim 112bl.

iStockphoto.com: DieterMeyrl 1, Olga_ Gavrilova 16clb, parys 21tl, powerofforever 58bl.

Kirsuberjatréð: 79tr.

National Museum of Iceland, ÞJÓÐMINJASAFN ÍSLANDS: 40cl.

Micro Bar: 60cra.

Photoshot: Stefan Auth 94tl; Picture Alliance/Carsten Schmidt 24br.

Rauða Húsið: 113tr.

Restaurant Reykjavík: 81cra.

Rex Features: Agencia EFE 69tr.

Reykjavík City Museum: G. Bjarki Gudmundsson 41br.

Rub23: 62bl.

Sigurjón Ólafsson Museum: Embrace - NATO, 1949, by Sigurjón Ólafsson LSÓ 1102 41tl.

Þrír Frakkar: Picasa 65cr.

Cover

Front and spine: **iStockphoto.com:** DieterMeyrl.

Back: **Dreamstime.com:** ristinn Kristinsson tr, Tawatchai Prakobkit crb, David Watts Jr. tl; **Getty Images:** L. Toshio Kishiyama cla; **iStockphoto.com:** DieterMeyrl.

Pull out map cover

iStockphoto.com: DieterMeyrl.

All other images © Dorling Kindersley
For further information see: www.dkimages.com

As a guide to abbreviations in visitor information blocks: **Adm** = admission charge; **D** = dinner; **L** = lunch.

FSC MIX
Paper from responsible sources
FSC™ C018179
www.fsc.org

DK | Penguin Random House

Printed and bound in China

First edition 2010

Published in Great Britain by Dorling Kindersley Limited 80 Strand, London WC2R 0RL

Published in the United States by DK US 1450 Broadway, Suite 801 New York, NY 10018, USA

Copyright © 2010, 2019 Dorling Kindersley Limited

A Penguin Random House Company

19 20 21 22 10 9 8 7 6 5 4 3 2

Reprinted with revisions 2012, 2014, 2016, 2018, 2019

A CIP catalogue record is available from the British Library.

A catalogue record for this book is available from the Library of Congress.

ISSN 1479-344X

ISBN 978-0-2413-6480-2

Phrase Book

Icelandic is a Nordic language. Many of its sounds do not exist in English, so the pronunciations below are for guidance only. Icelandic has three letters that do not exist in modern English: þ ("thorn", pronounced as th as in "thin"); ð ("eth", pronounced as soft th as in "the"); æ ("aye", pronounced as i as in "light"). Stress falls on the first syllable of the word.

Guidelines for Pronunciation

Vowels

There are seven vowels – a, e, i, o, u, y and æ, five of which take a stress accent, which changes the pronunciation. The "o" can have an umlaut over it.

a = as in "sat"
á = ow as in "owl"
e = as in "met"
i = as in "sit"
í = ee as in "feel"
o = as in "hot"
ó = as in "hole"
ö = "uh" sound
u = as in "put"
ú = oo as in "fool"
ý = ee as in "meet"
æ = i as in "light"

Letter combinations

Some combined letters in Icelandic have special pronunciations.

au = as o in "hole"
ei = as ai in "hail"
ey = as ai in "hail"
fn = as bn
ll = as tl
sj = as sh in "fish"
fl = as bl, but as fl at the start of a word
ng = as nk at the end of a word, as ng in the middle

In an Emergency

Help!	Hjálp!	hy-oulp
Call a doctor	Náið í lækni	nou-ith ee laek-ni
Call an ambulance	Hringdu í sjúkrabíl	hreen-du ee syoo-kra-beel
Call the police	Hringdu í lögregluna	hreen-du ee leu-rekl-una
Call the fire brigade	Hringdu í slökkviliðið	hreen-du ee sleuk-vi-lith-ith

Communication Essentials

Yes	Já	yow
No	Nei	nay
Please (offering)	Gjörðu svo vel	gyeurth-u svo vel
Thank you	Takk/takk fyrir	takk /takk fir-ir
Excuse me	Afsakið	af-sak-ith
Hello	Halló	hallo
Hello (polite)	Vertu sæl/sæll	vert-u sael(f.)/saetl(m.)
Goodbye	Bless	bless
Good night /morning /evening	Góða nótt /morgunn Gott kvöld	go-tha nott go-tha morg-un gott kveu-ld

Useful Phrases

How are you?	Hvað segirðu gott?	kvahth say-irth-u gott
Very well, thank you.	Allt gott	alht gott
That's fine.	Það er fínt/ gott	thath er feen-t/ gott
Where is/ are ...?	Hvar er/ eru ...?	kvar er/ eru
How do I get to ...?	Hvernig kemst ég til ...?	kvern-ig kem-st yieg til

Do you speak English?	Talarðu ensku?	tal-arth-u ensk-u
I don't understand.	Ég skil ekki	yieg skil ekki

Shopping

How much does this cost?	Hvað kostar þetta?	kvath kost-ar thett-a
I would like ...	Ég ætla að fá ...	yieg aetla ath fou
Do you take ... credit cards? traveller's cheques?	Takið þið ... kreditkort? ferðatékka?	tak-ith thith kre-dit-kort ferth-a-tiekk-a
What time do you open/ close?	Hvenær opnið þið/ lokið þið?	kven-aer oph-nith thith/ lok-ith thith?
this one	þessi hérna	thessi hier-nah
that one	þessi þarna	thessi thar-nah
expensive	dýrt	deer-t
size	stærð	sdaerth

Types of Shop

bakery	bakarí	ba-ka-ree
bank	banki	boun-ki
chemist	apótek	ap-o-tek
fishmonger	fiskibúð	fisk-i-booth
garage (mechanics)	bílaverkstæði	beel-a-verk-staeth-i
market	markaður	mark-ath-ur
post office	pósthús	post-hoos
supermarket	matarverslun	mah-dar-vers-lun
travel agent	ferðaskrifstofa	fertha-skrif-sdofa

Sightseeing

art gallery	listagallerí	list-ah-gall-er-ee
bay	flói	flo-i
beach	fjara	fyar-ah
bike	reiðhjól	raith-hyeeol
bus (town)	strætó	straeh-tou
bus (long dist.)	rúta	roo-ta
bus station	umferðami- ðstöð	um-fertha-mith- steuth
bus ticket	strætó/rútu miði	straeh-tou/roo-tu mithi
car	bíll	bee-dlh
car rental	bílaleiga	bee-la-laig-a
cathedral	dómkirkja	dom-kirk-ya
church	kirkja	kirk-ya
glacier	jökull	yeu-kudl
harbour	höfn	heubn
hot spring	hver	kver
island	eyja	ai-yah
lake	stöðuvatn	steu-thu-vatn
mountain	fjall	fyadlh
museum	safn	sabn
tourist information	upplýsinga- miðstöð	uph-lees-eenga- mith-sdeuth
waterfall	foss	foss

Staying in a Hotel

Do you have a vacant room?	Eigið þið laust herbergi?	aigith thith laost her-berg-i
double room with double bed	Tveggja manna herbergi með hjónarúmi	tvegg-ya mann-a her-berg-i meth hyonah-roommi
twin room	tveggja manna herbergi	tvegg-ya mann-a her-berg-i

single room	eins manns herbergi	ayns manns her-berg-i
room with bath/shower	herbergi með baði/sturtu	her-berg-i meth bath-i/sturh-ta
I have a reservation	Ég á pantað	yieg ou pant-ath

Eating Out

Have you got a table?	Eigið þið laust borð?	aigith thith laost borth
I'd like to reserve a table.	Gæti ég pantað borð.	gyaet-i yieg pant-ath borth
breakfast	morgunmatur	morg-un-mat-ur
lunch	hádegismatur	hou-deg-is-mat-ur
dinner	kvöldmatur	kveuld-mat-ur
The bill, please.	Reikninginn takk.	raikn-ing-inn takk
waitress/waiter	þjónn	thyo-dn
menu	matseðill	maht-seth-idl
starter	smáréttur	smou-riet-ur
first course	forréttur	for-riet-ur
main course	aðalréttur	athal-riet-ur
dessert	eftirréttur	eft-ir-riet-ur
wine list	vínlisti	veen-list-i
glass	glas	glas
bottle	flaska	flask-a
knife	hnífur	hneev-ur
fork	gaffall	gaff-adl
spoon	skeið	skaith

Menu Decoder

bjór	byorh	beer
brauð	braoth	bread
ferskir ávextir	fersk-ir ou-vekst-irh	fresh fruit
fiskur	fisk-ur	fish
franskar	fransk-ar	chips
grænmeti	graen-met-i	vegetables
grillað	grill-ath	grilled
gufusoðið	gu-fu-soth-ith	poached
hvítvín	kveet-veen	white wine
ís	ees	ice cream
kaka/ vínarbrauð	ca-ka/ veen-ar braoth	cake/ pastry
kartöflur	kart-eufl-ur	potatoes
kjöt	kyeut	meat
kjúklingur	kyook-leeng-ur	chicken
lambakjöt	lamb-ah-kyeut	lamb
laukur	laok-ur	onions
lax	laks	salmon
mjólk	myolk	milk
nautasteik	nao-ta-staik	beef
ostur	os-tur	cheese
pipar	phi-par	pepper
pylsa/ pulsa	pils-ah/ pul-sah	hotdog
rauðvín	raoth-veen	red wine
rækjur	rai-kyur	prawns
sjávarréttur	syou-va-rietd-ur	seafood
smjör	smyeurh	butter
soðið	soth-ith	boiled
sódavatn	so-da-vadn	mineral water
sósa	so-sa	sauce
steikt	staikt	fried
súkkulaði	sook-u-lath-i	chocolate
súpa	soo-ba	soup
svínakjöt	sveen-a-kyeut	pork

sykur	siik-ur	sugar
te	teh	tea
vatn	vahdn	water
ýsa	ee-sa	haddock

Useful Signs

open	opið	op-ith
closed	lokað	lohk-ath
entry	inn/inngangur	inn/inn-goung-ur
exit	út/útgangur	oot/oot-goung-ur
jeep track	jeppaslóð	yepp-ah-sloth
parking	bílastæði	bee-la-staeth-i
one-lane bridge	einbreið brú	ayn-braith broo
danger	hætta	haett-ah
forbidden	bannað	bann-ath
end of tarmac	malbik slitlag endar	mal-bik slit-lag end-ar
campsite	tjaldsvæði	tyald-svaethi
toilet	klósett	clo-sett
ladies' toilet	kvennaklósett	kvenn-a-clo-sett
gents' toilet	karlaklósett	karl-a-clo-sett

Time

one minute	ein mínúta	ayn meen-oot-a
one	ein	ayn
hour	klukkustund	kluk-u-stun-dh
a day	dagur	dag-ur
Monday	mánudagur	moun-u-dag-ur
Tuesday	þriðjudagur	thrith-yu-dag-ur
Wednesday	miðvikudagur	mith-vik-u-dag-ur
Thursday	fimmtudagur	flmt-u-dag-ur
Friday	föstudagur	feust-u-dag-ur
Saturday	laugardagur	laog-ar-dag-ur
Sunday	sunnudagur	sunnu-dag-ur

Numbers

1	einn	aydn
2	tveir	tvayr
3	þrír	threer
4	fjórir	fyor ir
5	fimm	fim
6	sex	segs
7	sjö	syeu
8	átta	outt-a
9	níu	nee-u
10	tíu	tee-u
11	ellefu	edl-ev-u
12	tólf	tolvh
13	þrettán	thrett-dyoun
14	fjórtán	fyorh-dyoun
15	fimmtán	fim-dyoun
16	sextán	segs-dyoun
17	sautján	sao-dyoun
18	átján	out-dyoun
19	nítján	nee-dyoun
20	tuttugu	tutt-ug-u
21	tuttugu og einn	tutt-ug-u og aydn
30	þrjátíu	thryou-tee-u
40	fjörtíu	fyeur-tee-u
50	fimmtíu	fim-tee-u
60	sextíu	segs-tee-u
70	sjötíu	syeu-tee-u
80	áttatíu	outt-a-tee-u
90	níutíu	nee-u-tee-u
100	hundrað	hund-rath
1000	þúsund	thoos-und
1,000,000	milljón	mil-ee-yon

Iceland Town Index

Reykjavík Selected Street Index